"You are doing something special fc ...... ing *Your Message Matters*. The investment of your time will come back multiplied with more confidence and enthusiasm—and you'll discover your own powerful message that will inspire and encourage others along the way."

**Dan Miller**, author of *48 Days to the Work You Love*

"To build a successful personal brand today, you need a platform. In *Your Message Matters*, Jonathan Milligan lays out a comprehensive four-step plan to help you turn your passion into a profitable online business. For aspiring writers, speakers, and coaches, this book is a game changer."

**Michael Hyatt**, *New York Times* bestselling author

"What is your WHAT? That is a question I've been challenging others with for the past decade. Milligan lays out a comprehensive framework to help you discover the three most essential ingredients for building a personal brand online today. In the pages of this book, you'll nail down your purpose, passion, and people. Now more than ever, this book is mandatory reading."

**Steve Olsher**, founder/editor-in-chief of *Podcast Magazine*; *New York Times* bestselling author of *What Is Your WHAT?*

"I'm a big believer in building a portable lifestyle business. In *Your Message Matters*, Jonathan demystifies the process of how to take your story, experience, or passion and turn it into a thriving online business. There's never been a better time to work from home doing what you love than right now."

**Natalie Sisson**, chief potentialist and two-time #1 bestselling author of *The Suitcase Entrepreneur* and *The Freedom Plan*

"Serving a tribe of people online can sustain your business for a lifetime. But how do you get started in the first place? Jonathan takes you on a journey from believing you have a message to defining what your message actually is to marketing your message for business success. This book is a must-read for any online entrepreneur."

**Stu McLaren**, founder of the TRIBE course and *Marketing Your Business* podcast

"Over the last decade, there has been an explosion of personal brand businesses online. Whether you want to write, speak, teach, or coach online, Jonathan has compiled the step-by-step roadmap to make that happen for you!"

Kary Oberbrunner, author of *Day Job to Dream Job*
and *Elixir Project*

"In a world full of pretenders and pseudogurus, Jonathan Milligan is the real deal. He shows you how to quickly stand out and be heard in a noisy world . . . and ultimately build a business and a life you love, just like he has done himself. I've watched him grow his business from scratch the same way he teaches in this book. Read it now!"

Matt McWilliams, host of *The Affiliate Guy* podcast

"Finding your one and only purpose in this life can be daunting. In this book, Jonathan unpacks in detail why we don't discover our purpose in life but rather uncover it. If you've been struggling with direction, this book will deliver!"

Jared Easley, co-founder, co-organizer, and VP of content
and community for Podcast Movement

"You have a message to share and an audience to serve. But it's easy to get stuck in the 'how.' In this inspiring and practical book, Jonathan walks you step-by-step through the process of uncovering your unique gift, discovering your ideal audience, and clarifying the problem your message solves. I highly recommend you grab a copy of this book! You'll find the practical worksheets and assessments you need to finally make progress and make a living sharing your message."

Brian Dixon, clarity coach and co-founder of hope*writers;
author of *Start with Your People*

"You have a message, and you deserve to have your message heard. Read Jonathan's book and you'll discover how to build multiple streams of income from your message. This book is ideal for speakers, writers, and coaches alike. Grab your copy today; you can thank me later."

Grant Baldwin, author of *The Successful Speaker*

# YOUR
## MESSAGE
# MATTERS

# YOUR
# MESSAGE
# MATTERS

How to **rise above** the noise
and get paid for what you know

# Jonathan Milligan

**BakerBooks**

*a division of Baker Publishing Group*
Grand Rapids, Michigan

© 2020 by Jonathan Milligan

Published by Baker Books
a division of Baker Publishing Group
PO Box 6287, Grand Rapids, MI 49516-6287
www.bakerbooks.com

Printed in the United States of America

Library of Congress Cataloging-in-Publication Data
Names: Milligan, Jonathan, 1976– author.
Title: Your message matters : how to rise above the noise and get paid for what you know / Jonathan Milligan.
Description: Grand Rapids, Michigan : Baker Books, [2020]
Identifiers: LCCN 2020015903 | ISBN 9781540900333 (paperback)
Subjects: LCSH: Success in business. | Entrepreneurship. | Motivation (Psychology) | Confidence.
Classification: LCC HF5386 .M64 2020 | DDC 658.4/5—dc23
LC record available at https://lccn.loc.gov/2020015903

ISBN 978-1-5409-0118-7 (hardcover)

The author is represented by The Christopher Ferebee Agency, www.christopherferebee.com.

20  21  22  23  24  25  26        7  6  5  4  3  2  1

This book is dedicated to my beautiful bride,

Charity,

who said I'd write a book one day.
You believed in me before I believed in myself.
Without your persistent encouragement,
this book never would have been written.

I love you.

# Contents

9

# Introduction

*"I'm just ready to go fail at something."*

I spoke those exact words to my coworker late one night in an empty parking lot. I had finished the night shift of my call center job, and I was exhausted.

My exhaustion wasn't from work, but from a more profound frustration in my life. Nine months prior I had quit my safe and secure job teaching at the local high school. Both of my parents are retired educators, so I had long assumed my life's work would be the same. After all, teaching is a great profession. You get the summers off, you are not called in to work on the weekends, and when your kids are off, so are you. But I was miserable at my high school teaching job. I loved to teach. I even had a great relationship with the students, but I couldn't shake the feeling that there was something else I might love even more. Something was stirring within my soul. I felt a calling for something specific to who I am. But I had no clue as to what it could be.

And so I made the difficult decision not to renew my teaching contract. Instead, I pursued the world of entrepreneurship.

Quitting my teaching job was no easy choice, especially with a young family at the time. Still, it felt like the right decision. My wife, Charity, and I had been married for just five years. Our daughter, Kayla, was two years old, and we were expecting a son, who we named Jordan. I felt the weight of responsibility on my shoulders to provide for my family. Was it even possible to find work I felt called to? Should I just focus on finding work that provided for my family instead? Was I just being selfish by trying to pursue a different line of work? Is there even a way to do both (provide for my family and do work I love)? Those were the deep questions I was wrestling with.

I landed a call center job at night to cover the monthly bills, which left my days free to launch a business of some kind. Nine months later, though, I had nothing to show for it. I'd read every business book, watched every online video, and bought every course that I thought could help, but I had zero results. I had done all of the research, but I felt stuck and unsure as to what to do next.

Have you been there? You decide to go hard after your dreams and end up drowning in a sea of information instead. That's what happened to me. Paralysis by analysis had set in. For months I'd thought *a little bit more information* was the secret to unlocking my success. If I knew everything, I couldn't fail, right?

Wrong. The fact is, learning is important, but it often gives us a false sense of progress. No one can ever learn their way to results in life. That hard reality was now settling in.

Then one night I let my frustration out with a coworker. "I'm just ready to go fail at *something*!" I was tired of feeling immobilized. I was finally ready for action, even if the result I got wasn't the one I wanted. Once I spoke those words, I knew I would never be the same. My situation didn't change, but my mindset shifted. The pain of not going after my dreams had become greater than the pain of failing at something.

So I decided to just get started. I first dabbled in real estate. My idea was to buy an undervalued property and make money fixing it up. I found a rundown single-family home in a decent neighborhood and purchased it. My days were spent running errands to Home Depot (way too many times I might add). My nights were spent clocking in at the call center so I could still pay the bills. Life was busy. A few months later, things finally began to pay off. I walked away with $12,000 in my pocket after a successful real estate sale. While I should have been ecstatic about my results, the biggest lesson I learned was that real estate was not my thing. I just didn't enjoy the construction and remodeling process.

I took the money I had earned from the property and used the funds to join a business start-up. Since the company was practically brand new, they couldn't offer me a salary. I would have to work on a 100 percent commission instead. The money we earned from the real estate sale would serve as my family's paycheck until I earned my first commission. The business was an executive search firm for accounting professionals. The crazy part is that I had no background in accounting and finance. But I stayed at that job for over seven years. I learned the ins and outs of career transition of accounting professionals. Still, I knew this wasn't my life's work.

## The Day Everything Changed

One day, almost by accident, I came across an old out-of-print book entitled *Acres of Diamonds*. Before it was made into a short book, it was first a lecture given by the founder of Temple University, Russell Conwell. In the book, Conwell shares the tale of an African farmer who searched for wealth and meaning. The man had heard stories of other settlers who had made millions discovering diamonds. Desiring to achieve the same, he sold his farm and spent the rest of his life traveling Africa in an unsuccessful attempt to find diamonds. Broke and depressed, he finally threw himself into a river and drowned.

Meanwhile, the man who had bought his farm was walking along on his property one day when he discovered an unusual stone in the creek bed. It turned out to be a diamond. On further investigation, he found the entire property was covered in beautiful diamonds. That land would become known as one of the world's richest diamond mines. If only its original owner had taken the time to cultivate his own land first, he would have found the millions he sought.[1]

The moral of the story is this: finding your purpose in life is not an *external* pursuit but an *inward* journey. You don't find your purpose in life; you uncover it. Like a diamond in a mine. As Swiss psychologist Carl Jung advised, "Your vision will become clear only when you look into your heart. Who looks outside, dreams. Who looks inside, awakens."[2]

And there it was in black and white. My life was like the African farmer who was only focused on his external pursuit of purpose and happiness. He mistakenly thought he'd find his purpose out there somewhere. I had finally discovered a profound truth that would alter the trajectory of my life. The truth I found was this: my purpose was right under my nose all along. My purpose would reveal itself once I uncovered what was unique about me—*my* hidden diamond.

Through a series of self-discovery exercises that I'll walk you through later in the book, my hidden diamond (what we'll refer to as your unique gift) began to be revealed. My unique gift was "resourcefulness." The way I best expressed this gift was through teaching. Not traditional teaching, but teaching in a new, creative way that I'll show you in this book. Once I made this discovery, I immediately thought, *Now what? How do I apply my unique gift to work I'm passionate about?* I didn't know it at the time, but I needed a *message*. What I would later come to discover is that a message combines three things: purpose, passion, and people.

At the time, I was passionate about helping people find a better job. The people I could best serve at the time were accounting professionals. The only thing missing from the equation was me being able to fully utilize my unique gift—me, being a resourceful teacher.

I found the answer to my problem in launching a career advice blog. It was the perfect outlet for my resourcefulness. I could write career-related articles, create online courses to sell, and offer coaching services. I was doing none of these things at the time because in the traditional model of executive recruiting you only earned money when you placed a candidate in a new job. Besides, I wanted to build my own business where I could work from anywhere.

But there was still a problem. As I mentioned earlier, I'm not an accountant. I didn't even take accounting in college. *Who am I to go off on my own and build a business advising accountants?* I wondered. My lack of confidence was holding me back from going after my dreams.

That's when I discovered a secret that is the premise of this entire book.

> Confidence comes from the deep belief
> that the world needs your message.

Simply put, *your message matters*. Big or small, if your message has the power to change someone's day—or life—you have a responsibility to share it. Doubts vanish, delays diminish, and distractions fade when we focus on our message. When we focus our attention on ourselves, doubt creeps in. But placing our focus on our message increases our confidence.

Drawing from this newfound confidence, I finally launched that career advice blog in 2009. It wasn't perfect, especially in the beginning, but I was starting to finally lean into my purpose. By tapping into my resourcefulness, I published a few career-related articles each and every week. After a few months, I started receiving emails from people across the country and even around the world who had read and benefited from my articles. That's when I decided to take it a step further. I created an online course that allowed me to teach others how to go from designing a resume to negotiating a salary. Before too long, the online course was up for sale on my blog. From there, I began to discover other ways to earn money from this blog—many of which I'll also teach you in this book. When it was all said and done, by 2011 I had built an online career advice blog into a business with twelve income streams. I was able to leave my day job and work full-time from home. The best part was that most of the income streams didn't require my time and attention. I was no longer trading time for dollars. I had a business I loved that also gave me the freedom I so desperately wanted.

Next, I took the same business-building principles I had learned from the first blog and applied them to building a second successful online business brand. Applying these principles in a new setting proved to me beyond a doubt what I already knew: these principles work.

Now I want to teach you how to do the same. You're reading this right now because you have a stirring deep within. You know you have more to give. You know you have more to contribute. Maybe you already have a story, passion, skill, or experience you'd love to turn into a business. Perhaps you're not even sure what your message is yet. Either way, this book is your roadmap to making things happen.

## The Amazing Opportunity That Exists for All of Us

This time in world history is special for lots of reasons. The world has drastically changed in the last two decades. It's changed so fast, though, that many of us are unaware of the new opportunities in front of us. Opportunities that were once impossible for most people are now available to everyone. The playing field of building a business is now more level than ever before. Before the dawn of the internet, advertising (or, put in another way, messaging) was primarily controlled by big companies with large advertising budgets. If you wanted to get your message out and build a business two decades ago, your options were to spend a lot of money, spend a lot of time, or do both. Examples of old, expensive methods of advertising include

- TV commercials
- radio advertising
- direct mail campaigns
- networking
- newspaper advertising

Under the old advertising model, the business with the biggest advertising budget won. Large companies got larger while smaller start-ups struggled to get their message out.

Then, the internet changed everything. It was a seismic shift that went unnoticed by most of society. Only a handful of online entrepreneurs noticed the change. The ones who noticed were able to grow their following, income, and impact quickly.

In his book *Dotcom Secrets*, author Russell Brunson describes a marketing seminar he attended at a local Holiday Inn that opened his eyes to the new opportunity. Russell noticed that "instead of using mail, they were using email; instead of using magazines, they had blogs; instead of the radio, they were using podcasts. It was fascinating, I was hooked from day one."[3]

Almost overnight, the new media had burst onto the scene. Just look in the following table at the difference between the old media versus the new media of today.

| Old Media (High Financial Cost) | New Media (Little to No Cost) |
| --- | --- |
| TV shows (or commercials) | YouTube channel |
| radio shows | podcast show |
| direct mail campaign | email list broadcast |
| networking | social media networking |
| newspapers | blog posts |

Today, anyone with a message can build a platform from the comfort of their own home.

- Want to start a TV show? Launch your own YouTube channel.
- Want to be a radio host? Start a podcast show.
- Want to broadcast a sales message? Send an email to your list.
- Want to network with others? Leverage social media outlets.
- Want to build a newspaper readership? Launch a blog.

The point is that you already have access to everything you need to be successful. All you are in need of is a roadmap—a step-by-step plan that has proven to work across industries, personalities, and geographical locations. That's what this book will provide. In the pages ahead, you'll hear stories of ordinary people who are leveraging today's media to build their business. You'll discover how

- a bread truck deliveryman from Milwaukee built an international marketing agency
- a college dropout built a Fortune 5000 business in just five years sharing his advice online

- a camera-shy woman grew a seven-figure online education business about livestreaming
- a struggling young man and formerly suicidal teenager turned his mess into his message and became a bestselling author
- a burned-out corporate employee left her day job to travel the world (all while running a business from her laptop)

We live in a fantastic time. Anyone anywhere can influence anyone anywhere. With a laptop and a Wi-Fi connection, you can run a profitable business online—no matter the location. Wow, how times have changed. Before the internet, you had to physically move to take advantage of opportunity. Whether it was the Gold Rush of the 1850s or the Second Industrial Revolution of the early 1900s, opportunity was always location dependent. Think about the music industry. For decades aspiring singers have moved to Nashville, Tennessee, with the hope of being "discovered." Many became waiters and waitresses to pay the bills, while doing what they really love on the weekends: singing. But today, you don't have to move to Nashville to get noticed.

A recent article from *Become Singers* listed the top ten singers who got famous through YouTube. A few of those singers include Justin Bieber, Carly Rae Jepsen, Greyson Chance, Cody Simpson, and Tori Kelly.[4] It's true: anyone anywhere can influence people everywhere.

- It doesn't matter where you live.
- It doesn't matter what's on your resume.
- It doesn't matter what credentials you have or don't have.
- It doesn't matter how young or old you are.
- It doesn't matter how successful you've been in life.

If all this is true, then what is required to get started? In order to launch the business of your dreams, there are only two requirements.

First, you must believe you have a message to share. I'm often surprised at how many people discount their experience, skills, or story. They don't see the gold mine of opportunity in front of them. You *do* have a message; you just need to uncover it.

Second, you must believe that your message *matters*.

That's it.

You probably have many questions at this point; that's okay. In the pages ahead, we will walk you through a proven roadmap to help you put all of the pieces together. All I'm asking of you is to be willing to go on the journey with me.

Let's begin.

# PART 1

# BELIEVE YOUR MESSAGE

"Writing is not your thing. Don't become a writer." I heard those words in my freshman year of college from the English professor. Creative Writing 101 was one of the few college classes I enjoyed. But I couldn't seem to score higher than a C on most of my stories.

I set my dream of writing on the shelf.

Words have power and can shape your identity if you let them. And I did. Actually, I let *one person's* opinion tell me that I wasn't a writer—my college professor's. And I lived with the effects of that for a long time.

"You're going to write a book someday!"

Not long after we married, my wife said those words to me. At the time, I couldn't have been any further away from being able to make her declaration come true. For one thing, my writing dream was dead. But that wasn't the only problem.

I had no audience.

I had no experience.

I had no manuscript.

I had no book idea.

I wasn't a professional writer.

As far as I was concerned, I was in the wrong place at the wrong time to become a professional writer, and I was going in the wrong direction if I wanted to make it happen. I'd even skipped typewriting class in high school to take yearbook instead. To this day, I still don't set my fingers on the home row while typing. My writing dream seemed completely dead. But words are powerful. My wife's words that day set in my heart a belief that I could be a writer someday.

Fifteen years later, I had forgotten that she'd said those words to me. It was a spring day in March of 2015, and the first copy of my first book had showed up in my mailbox. There's nothing like holding your own published book in your hands for the first time. I handed it to my wife, and tears fell from her eyes as she held the book. She looked at me and said, "I told you . . . you'd write a book someday." And then the memory flooded back. I remembered her saying the words. And she had been right. I had written a book, just as she'd predicted.

It was a special moment we shared together.

For over twenty years, I had let one person's opinion carry too much weight in my life. I had let my college professor's words dictate my future and my calling. Thankfully, my wife's words later had a positive effect that overrode that message. But I had lost many years when I could have been writing, all because I trusted someone else's opinion more than I trusted what I felt inside. Don't let the discouraging words of others become an anchor to your soul.

Pushing past fear and stepping forward with confidence is something that's easier said than done. Have you ever been excited about a new idea only to have the wind knocked out of your sails by another person? That's precisely how Ryan, a reader of my blog, felt. He said it this way: "What do you do when a lack of verbal confirmation from others sucks the wind out of your sails before you've even had a chance to lift the anchor?"

Our message is our sailboat; the high seas are the exciting adventure that awaits. One negative forecast by a bystander causes us to question the mission. We begin to think safety is better than adventure. That playing it safe is better. The problem with this line of thinking, though, is that the pain of experience weighs in ounces, but the pain of regret weighs in tons.

How do we overcome those feelings of inadequacy, especially when we feel like we don't belong? How do we balance those feelings with the burning desire to get our message out so we can help more people? Maybe we feel a lot like Susan, one of my survey respondents, who said, "How do I quiet the inner self-critic who tells me I'm not the right person for the job?"

If you struggle with doubt, you are not alone. Suzy Kassem, an American writer and philosopher, says it best: "Doubt kills more dreams than failure ever will."[1] If you think about it, most of us don't fear doubt. What we fear most is failing. But if what Suzy Kassem tells us is true, doubt is the more reasonable fear. Too often we treat doubt as a sign *not* to do something. But what if the reverse were true? What if at the first sign of doubt we recognized the need to take bold action instead? How different would our lives be if we treated doubt, not failure, as the dream killer?

But how do we overcome doubt on a consistent basis? The only way to kill doubt is to grab hold of confidence. The more courage we display, the less doubt holds us back from being our best.

Dan Sullivan, founder of Strategic Coach, says, "Protecting and cultivating your confidence is your number one responsibility as an entrepreneur because confidence is the ability that activates all other abilities."[2] For many of us, confidence in ourselves seems impossible. We know our shortcomings. We know where we lack self-discipline. We know we don't have everything together. So how can we live with confidence without feeling like an imposter? As a not-yet-successful writer, I was struggling with all these same thoughts and questions.

But as you'll learn in part 1, confidence comes when you *believe* your message matters. What you're about to discover is that confidence is not about the messenger at all. It's about the message. Let's get started.

# 1

# What Exactly Is a Messenger?

In his modern-day parable, *The Dream Giver*, Bruce Wilkinson tells the tale of a character named Ordinary, who lives in the Land of Familiar. Each morning Ordinary gets up to go to his Usual Job. In the evenings after dinner, he sits in his recliner and stares at the box that mesmerizes most Nobodys. Every day is an exact copy of the day before. Ordinary seems content with his daily routines. He is content with life and finds it to be reliable and predictable. That is until the day everything changes. Bruce Wilkinson describes it like this: "Ordinary noticed a small, nagging feeling that something big was missing from his life. Or maybe the feeling was that he was missing from something big. He wasn't sure."[1]

Later in the story, Ordinary discovers that the nagging feeling is his big dream, tugging at him to be noticed. At first, this realization excites him. The thought of going after his big dream gives purpose to his life. Yet Ordinary has a big problem: the dream inside of him is too big for an Ordinary like himself.[2]

Can you relate? Do you have a small, nagging feeling inside that maybe something is missing in your life? Maybe, like Ordinary, you're not even sure exactly what it is. That's okay. All you need to build the business of your dreams is to answer four fundamental questions:

- What is your unique gift?
- Who do you want to help?
- What problem will you solve?
- How will you attract the people you can help to your business?

I will help you answer each of these four questions in the pages ahead. After following the plan laid out in this book, you'll know with confidence what is the right path forward for you. You'll be ready to begin your work as a messenger. But before we jump into action, we must answer an important question: What exactly is a messenger?

## The Eight Attributes of a Messenger

As you go through the book, you'll hear two terms I use often: *messenger* and *message-based business*. Assuming these concepts may be new for you, let's define them both now.

First, the term *messenger*. A messenger is anyone who has a passion, message, skill, or story to share with the world. In other words, you have a desire to influence others with information and advice that can help them be successful.

Second, the term *message-based business*, another phrase we will be using throughout the book. A message-based business earns income through the selling of information, instruction, and advice. A few examples include online courses, membership sites, speaking engagements, coaching programs, books, and events. A message-based business is ideal for those who want to write, coach, teach, or speak for a living. In chapter 14, I'll share with you twelve different ways you can get paid to share your message.

But how do you know if you want to be a messenger or even build a message-based business to begin with? After carefully observing this still fairly new and growing industry, I've discovered some attributes that are common to all messengers. To be clear, you don't need to possess all eight attributes to qualify. If any are true for you, then this is the business for you. Read through the following list of eight attributes and place a check mark by those that resonate with you.

### 1. Messengers are creatively driven.

Messengers are wired to create. They can't escape their desire to be creative. They actually feel *called* to create. When it comes to their daily calendar, they love seeing zero appointments. It's not because they are antisocial. They just see an empty calendar as a blank canvas. They dream of having total creative freedom to express their thoughts and ideas. That creative urge can be expressed in many different ways. In my work, I often see it come to life in four ways: writing, speaking, coaching, and teaching.

### 2. Messengers are mission oriented.

Messengers wake up each day on a mission. They serve a cause greater than just personal survival. A messenger often sees the potential in others before they see it in themselves. While most of society is working for the weekends, messengers are working for a mission they deeply believe in.

### 3. Messengers are transformation makers.

Working hard just to earn a living doesn't appeal to most messengers. They are more deeply motivated by the prospect of causing change in the world and the lives of others. Income with no impact leaves an uncomfortable emptiness in the life of a messenger; they want the double win of both earning an income and making an impact. A messenger intends to work on things that make a difference in people's lives.

### 4. Messengers are challenge seekers.

Messengers get bored with living in the comfort zone of life. Comfort equals boredom for many of them. They aren't reckless or delusional, but they do view new challenges as exciting. They know the best fruit is found out on the end of the limb. While messengers may sometimes doubt their abilities, they still know that the undiscovered path is more exciting than the beaten-down trail.

### 5. Messengers are gift cultivators.

Messengers feel a curiosity about human potential. First, they desire to cultivate their own gifts. They want to live to their full potential. They love the insights they learn from personality tests and self-evaluation assessments. They enjoy becoming more self-aware and making new discoveries about their own personality and strengths. But messengers also enjoy unlocking new insights for others. They want other people to live to their full potential, and they want to help. At times, they may even want to see change in others more than others want change for themselves. This is because most messengers see their primary role as the guide, not the hero. They desperately want those they influence to step into the hero role they were meant to live.

### 6. Messengers are leading learners.

While learning and education end after college for most people, messengers are lifelong learners. They possess an intense desire to grow, learn, and be better. They consume books, watch courses, and attend events on topics in which they have an interest. Messengers can't help but turn around and teach what they've learned. Teaching is the ultimate form of learning for them. Being a leading learner keeps them fresh, engaging, and relevant.

### 7. Messengers are freedom lovers.

Messengers don't readily accept the status quo. Because they are change-makers, they often see the status quo as confining and conforming. Instead of believing this is *just the way things are*, they see how things can be better. They are on a crusade for freedom. High performance expert Brendon Burchard explains it this way in his book *The Motivation Manifesto*: "We are all meant to be wild and independent and free, our hearts filled with a ferocious passion for life. The day is meant to be ours, and our purpose within it is to live as who we truly are and enjoy the full terrain of life's freedom as we chase our own meaning and purpose, our own legacy."[3] Messengers want people who feel stuck to know there is a better way to live—that there is a way to break out of their constraints and live a life of freedom.

### 8. Messengers are future focused.

While most people focus on the challenges of today, messengers dwell on the possibilities of tomorrow. They often wonder, *How could life be different tomorrow if we just change what we are doing today?* Messengers inspire others to lift their heads, cast their eyes on the horizon, and stand in the future to see what could be.

How many of these eight statements resonate with you? If you see glimpses of yourself or your desires in these statements, then you are in the right place. Sure, you may have more questions than answers right now, but that's about to change. In the pages ahead, I'll help you clarify your message and then show you how to build an amazing business helping others.

## When Staying the Same Is Not an Option

What Ordinary felt inside was the stirring of his big dream. To get to the land of promise, he had to leave the Land of Familiar. To leave the Land of Familiar, he had to get past the Border Bullies blocking his path. To his surprise, the Border Bullies were not strangers, but people he knew: "He never imagined they'd be some of the Nobodies who knew him best! Now his Mother, Uncle, and Best Friend all stood silently before him, blocking his view of the bridge to his Big Dream. How would he ever get past them? Should he even try? He needed time to think."[4]

Most creative entrepreneurs feel a lot like Ordinary. They feel isolated with a big dream inside them. I know I did. No one else quite gets the vision we see. Where we see an opportunity, our friends see demise. They don't want to see us get hurt. They don't want to lose something important—*us*. But what they fail to realize is that staying the same is already killing us. It's a slow death of the soul. We were born with a purpose, calling, or deep mission to pursue. Our high sea calls. We must answer.

But before you get started on the *how*, you must believe, like Ordinary, that your dream is worth it. That's what we'll unpack next.

# 2

# Why Your Message Matters

Surviving as an immigrant to the United States in the mid-1800s was no easy feat. Surviving as a deaf-mute child made the challenge even greater. But that was the reality faced by Andrew Clemens. Due to contracting encephalitis as a young child, Andrew had lost the ability to hear and speak.

One day Andrew was playing among the cliffs and shallow caves in Iowa. He became fascinated by the different colors of sand. Each layer of the cliff had a unique color. Andrew began to experiment with this sand. He separated the grains of sand by color. Then Andrew began to layer the different colors of sand inside old chemist bottles he found. (These bottles are comparable to wine bottles we have today.) Over time, his artwork became more and more sophisticated. Using no glue, he created beautiful images of such subjects as George Washington, the American flag, and steamboats. Want to be in awe? Search online for Andrew Clemens artwork. You won't believe what you see. People far and wide began to pay Andrew for his bottles. Andrew Clemens had invented a new art form: sand art.[1]

## Four Important Reasons Your Message Matters

The fact is, your message matters. The world needs you to chase your talents. That's because the world will be a better place with them, just as it's a better place with the artwork of Andrew Clemens in it. We need you to pursue your gifts. Your gift is needed in the world. Your journey begins today.

When we look closer at the life of Andrew Clemens, we find four truths we can apply to our lives, and those truths point us to an important revelation: your message matters for four important reasons.

### 1. You have a gift.

Everyone is born with a gift. You were born with the seed of greatness. But it's up to you to grow it, nurture it, and use it to make a difference in the world. As Leo Buscaglia said, "Your talent is God's gift to you. What you do with it is your gift back to God."[2] Andrew Clemens's life is a perfect illustration of this. Even though it seemed at first as though Andrew didn't have much of a future, there was a unique gift buried inside him. Ultimately, curiosity led to passion, passion led to skill, and skill led to the value of his work in the world. Unfortunately, most of us today are too busy to slow down and become curious. Curiosity leads to great questions like

- What comes easily to me but is difficult for others?
- What am I doing when I feel the most alive?
- What value do I bring to every situation?
- Where can I make the biggest contribution to others?

Getting curious—actively wondering—is only the first step in uncovering your gift. You must also get outside perspective. We discount our gifts. We overlook our abilities.

I dismissed my unique gift for years. I set it aside and instead went on a journey to find my great purpose. *It must be lurking out there somewhere*, I figured. *I just need to try harder to find it.* But what I failed to realize is that I had it in me all along.

Maybe you feel that way too. You look at your life and doubt your abilities. You doubt that greatness exists inside you. That's why we need others to help us uncover what is great about us. You have immense value to share with the world. Your purpose in life is to uncover it and use it. You have a gift. Here's a promise I make to you: if you're willing to go on a journey with me, we'll uncover your unique gift together.

### 2. Your gift is needed in the world.

There is a mission in this life that only you can embark on. You were born at the right time in history. You were raised in the right geographical part of the earth. You live in the right generation in human history. Your gift is needed in the world.

The goal is not to become famous. The goal is to steward your gift, to make a difference in the world, to do what you were born to do. It's a longing that is found in every human heart. It might be buried, but it is there. You have value, and your value is sought after in the world.

You are a beautiful creation of God. You may only see the weaknesses, blemishes, and shortcomings. You may ask yourself, *Why would anyone follow me when I don't even have my own life together?* But that state of being—of not having it all together—is exactly what makes you attractive.

At times, my life feels like a complete mess too. I've changed careers more times than the average person. I've never found work in the field I originally studied for in college. I've started businesses that never got off the ground. If you judged my life based on my resume, you'd come to the conclusion that I'm a complete mess. On the surface I might look like a wandering child who doesn't know what he wants in life. Yet, somehow, I'm exactly where I'm supposed to be. And so are you. In times like these, there's only one thing to do: turn your mess into your message.

Andrew Clemens did just that. No, life was not easy for a deaf-mute child growing up in the Civil War era. But instead of focusing on what he lacked, Andrew made the most of what he had. Working from a place of seeming disability, he used old bottles and colorful sand to create something valuable for the world. If you were to look at the label placed on the bottom of one of his bottles, you'd find something fascinating: each bottle was signed "Andrew Clemens, Deaf-Mute." Now this isn't a phrase that is used much today, but the point is this: Andrew Clemens wanted people to know that he'd risen above his circumstances and that seeming limitations hadn't stopped him and didn't have to be limiting for others either. People of all abilities can create something of tremendous beauty. He turned his tragedy into his brand. Your gift is no less important, and the world needs it too.

### 3. Living a full life is better than living a long life.

Andrew Clemens only lived to be thirty-seven years of age, but his life is still being talked about today. There's an argument to be made that living a full life is better than living a long life. I know I'd rather have a short, full life spent living my message than a long life wasted by wondering what might have been. The goal of life is not to avoid pain, live in comfort, and arrive safely at death. Rather, the goal of life is to live our purpose, share our passion, and make a difference in people. Your best times are not behind you. They are ahead of you. Live this one and only life to the fullest.

### 4. People are waiting for your dream to become a reality.

Before Andrew Clemens made it, the world didn't even know it needed sand art. But he both invented it and made a career out of it. He sold his finished bottles for five to seven dollars each. Once you factor in inflation, that would be the equivalent of about $157 each today. The world didn't know it needed sand art until sand art existed. And then it couldn't get enough of it.

As his artwork became more well known, custom orders increased. People saw value in his gift and were willing to spend the money to get one of his finished bottles. His sand art bottles are still sold in auctions today. In 2018, one of Andrew's bottles sold for $132,000 at an auction in Cincinnati, Ohio.[3]

Andrew had every right to give in to his challenges. He could have believed the limitations others placed on him. Instead, he decided to give himself over to courage instead of fear. He decided to explore his gift instead of bury it. He didn't know it then, but people had been waiting for his dream to become a reality. This same is true for you, my friend. People are waiting for what you have to give.

## The Day Walt Disney's Dream Almost Died

Believe it or not, Walt Disney once had a movie executive laugh out loud at his dream. Early in his career, Disney came across an opportunity of a lifetime. He had negotiated an appointment with one of the largest movie executives at the time, Louis B. Mayer. Walt planned to show Mayer his seven-minute Mickey Mouse cartoon in the hope that he could secure a contract. His dream was to bring his cartoon animations to movie theaters across the United States. Walt was optimistic about this particular meeting. He knew he had invented something revolutionary that everyone would want.

What happened next surprised him. Mayer didn't laugh at the cartoon; instead he laughed at Disney's dream. Not only did he push the button to turn off the projector during the cartoon, but he went on to tell Walt all of the reasons why his idea would never work. In so many words, the movie executive said that kids are afraid of mice and moms don't love them all that much either. No one, he said, is going to pay to watch a silly mouse. With that, he laughed and stormed out of the theater, while Walt stood there in embarrassment.

Has anyone ever laughed at your dream? Has anyone ever dismissed your life's message? If so, you're not alone. In fact, if you're reading this, you're in the right place. So what did Walt do in this situation? He decided to move forward anyway. Instead of giving up or allowing one person's opinion to carry too much weight on his dream, Walt persisted.

Within days he secured a meeting with a small but growing studio named Columbia Pictures. Frank Capra, Columbia's leading director, agreed to meet with Walt, but he was unenthusiastic about the meeting from the start. He was even less enthused at his first impression of Walt, describing him as a "scrawny, nondescript, hungry-looking young man, wearing two days' growth of beard and a slouch cap."[4]

But once the cartoon hit the screen, everything changed. Capra was so impressed with the cartoon that he insisted Harry Cohen, the head of Columbia Pictures, view it immediately. Walt signed a contract that day to produce a new cartoon every month for Columbia Pictures. While Walt still faced many business challenges in the days ahead, this single meeting produced enough monthly cash flow to keep Walt Disney Studios alive.[5]

If we, like Walt, have any chance of keeping the dream alive, we need to develop the courage to move forward, no matter what other people say. There are three things to keep in mind that can help you to do this:

### 1. Recognize that not everyone will understand your message.

Some of the most significant accomplishments that happened in the world in our lifetime once seemed impossible to many people.

Still, there were a few who believed in the dream. They believed a man could walk on the moon. They believed it was possible to hold a device in one's hand and talk with anyone around the world. They believed in the seemingly impossible.

Don't allow one person's opinion to shut down your dream. Not everyone will understand your message. It's your job to believe in your message even when others don't. What if Disney had given up on his dream that day? What if he had allowed one person's opinion to become his reality? There would be no Mickey Mouse, and there would be no Disneyland or Walt Disney World. Think about how much joy so many people would have missed out on. Getting negative feedback should not be a reason to pack it up and go home. You are going to need to believe in your message even when others don't.

### 2. Surround yourself with others who believe in your message.

While it may feel noble to charge ahead alone, you're going to need message carriers along the way. Message carriers are other people who catch the vision of what you are trying to do.

Walt Disney had his brother Roy. Roy's talent was in the numbers side of the business. Roy worked on financing the dream while Walt focused on the creative side. There were also Disney employees who caught the vision. In the early days, animators worked for Walt without pay because they believed in the dream so much. They worked nights and weekends to get the cartoon done. Walt had inspired them. They had a mission and message to get out to the world. All this hard work eventually paid off for these animators, enabling them to pursue dreams of their own. They were there in total support of Walt's vision.

How about you? Are there message carriers in your life you've taken for granted? If so, thank them for their unwavering support.

### 3. Focus on those waiting for your dream to become a reality.

What, then, gets us through the valley when our message takes a direct hit from others? Remembering what and who we're doing this for. Your message survives when you focus on those waiting for your dream to become a reality. There are people waiting for you to pursue your life's message. They need your advice, perspective, solution, or product. Whether you have what's needed to change someone's day or what's needed to change someone's life, it's important for you to make your dream a reality. We are waiting for you. There is a dream only you can fulfill. Your message matters.

## A Message from the Future

It was the night before my live event in Jacksonville, Florida, and attendees had flown in from all over to attend this two-day workshop. I was sitting in the hotel room finishing up the last few slides when a sudden thought occurred to me. What if I played my very first YouTube video for the live audience? That way they could see just how bad I was on camera when I first started.

We all tend to have a false belief that experts have this secret magic that turns everything they do into gold. But my first YouTube video was awful, period. My hope was that by showing them my first video, I would help them to push past fear and just get started. I went searching way back into the archives of my account and finally arrived at my very first YouTube video. What I saw next stunned me.

The publication date of my very first video was June 21, 2009. The opening day of my live event was June 21, 2019. The exact same day, just ten years apart.

I began to think, *What if I had listened to all those voices of fear and doubt and decided not to hit Publish that day?* Was that moment of courage back in June 21, 2009, what had led to a room full of people wanting to learn from me a decade later?

Being a fan of the movie *Back to the Future*, I thought, *What if I could hop in the DeLorean and set the date for June 21, 2009? What would I say to my younger self?* I decided I would probably tap him on the shoulder and say, "Be brave. People getting the help they need in the future depends on your courage in this moment. You've got this." I would encourage my younger self to demonstrate a thing I call "present courage," and I'm encouraging you to tap into it too.

## The Power of Present Courage

Every business you admire can be traced back in time to a moment of present courage. That single solitary act of signing the lease, buying the domain name, or turning the closed sign over to read "Open for business." Walt Disney started his animation studio in the loft of a barn. Jeff Bezos began Amazon in the garage of a rented home in Bellevue, Washington. Apple computers was founded by two college dropouts, Steve Jobs and Steve Wozniak, who started building the first Apple computer in Jobs's garage. That was in 1976. Today, I'm writing this book on one of their inventions.

If you are going to get your message into the world, you'll need to have *present courage*. In fact, the people you most want to help are just on the other side of your courage. To get a mental visual of what I mean, picture yourself standing next to a twenty-foot-high brick wall. There's a single rope hanging down in front of you. You have a hunch that what you want most in life, your big dream, is just on the other side of the wall. The problem is that you can't see it. You have no idea what's waiting for you on the other side of the wall.

On top of that, scaling the wall with the rope feels dangerous and scary. But what if there were thousands of people rooting for you to climb over that wall of courage? What if the people just on the other side of that wall represented your future fans and customers? What if you could hear them cheering you on? That's what I mean when I say that the people you most want to help are just on the other side of your courage. John Wayne famously said, "Courage is feeling the fear and saddling up anyways."[6] You may be thinking, *That's easy for John Wayne to say, but what about little old me? I'm not as talented or as well equipped as others.*

But courage comes when we learn to make do with what we have. When we step forward not because of but despite what we may personally lack. Follow any great feat in history, and you'll discover a profound truth. The prize doesn't always go to the fastest, smartest, and strongest. Sometimes it goes to those who possess immense courage.

While Martin Luther King Jr. is most known for his *I Have a Dream* speech (and for good reason), one of my favorite speeches of his is a sermon he preached to his own congregation. In an effort to strengthen their resolve, he prayed, "Lord, help me to accept my tools. However dull they are, help me to accept them. And then Lord, after I have accepted my tools, then help me to set out and do what I can do with my tools."[7]

Displaying present courage is not about having access to the best tools or having all of our skills perfected. Courage is about stepping forward with what we have because the mission is that important.

## Shift the Focus Away from Yourself

Have you noticed just how hard life is when you focus on yourself? To display present courage you must shift the focus away from yourself. For example, public speaking is nerve-racking if these are the kinds of thoughts you have in your head:

- How can I get the audience to like me?
- Do they think I'm funny?
- I hope they agree with the points I'm trying to get across.
- Do they think I'm a good speaker or a boring one?

Notice how all these statements include *me* or *I*. When you focus on yourself, the ego is in charge. When the ego is in charge, we've misplaced our priorities. We've mistakenly placed the focus on our own emotional comfort. Real confidence, however, comes when we place our focus on our message, not on ourselves.

This is good news for those of us who don't enjoy the spotlight. It's not about you. It's all about the message and its end result—the transformation of others. It's all about serving others. The world is not in need of another celebrity. The world *is* in need of more transformation. Everything becomes easier when we intentionally shift the focus away from ourselves. When we stop copying others, embrace our unique selves, and stop doubting ourselves, the critics lose their power over us. Life is best lived when we shift our focus away from ourselves.

## See Excuses as Lies You Tell Yourself

One day I wrote on a sticky note a line I first heard from bestselling author Robert Kiyosaki.[8] "Excuses are lies you tell yourself." I placed the sticky note on my computer monitor to be constantly reminded of this truth. It's amazing how many excuses race through our thoughts daily. *I don't have time to build my own business. I'm not a very good writer. Who am I to get paid to share my advice with others?* What's even more amazing is how easily we believe them. Why don't we challenge our excuses? I believe it's because to believe differently would require us to change. Think about it. Most of us live comfortable lives. We have a place to sleep, food in the pantry, and a bed to sleep in. Life is good. Yet there is still a stirring within us. Why? Because the goal was never comfort to begin with. We want to live a life that matters.

What I've discovered is that excuses are just false assumptions. They are often not based in truth. They are based in fear. Try this little experiment: The next time you feel an excuse pop into your head, write the words out on paper. Once you do, you'll likely have one of two reactions. You will either laugh or get mad. You may laugh at how silly the words sound when you see them written out in front of you. Or you may get angry. Frustration may arise as you think of how many times you've given in to that one lie. The good news is that you can change.

Change your thinking and your actions will change too. Best-selling author Steven Pressfield calls this "turning pro." Turning pro involves asking a simple question: If you were the best in the world at what you do, how would you behave? In his book *Turning Pro*, Pressfield writes:

> When we turn pro, everything becomes simple. Our aim centers on the ordering of our days in such a way that we overcome the fears that have paralyzed us in the past. . . . This changes our days completely. It changes what time we get up and it changes what time we go to bed. It changes what we do and what we don't do. It changes the activities we engage in and with what attitude we engage in them.[9]

The opposite of turning pro is believing your own excuses. Our excuses are born of the assumption that we aren't the best in the world at what we do. But you are the best at bringing your message to the world. In order to have present courage, you must see excuses as what they are: just lies you tell yourself. Thankfully, growth can happen quickly once you embrace this truth.

## Measure Your Actions, Not Your Results

I want results now! Have you ever said that? I know I have. We live in a world where people expect instant results. We want what we want, immediately. We simply put too much pressure on ourselves to see results now.

One of the biggest myths in business is the idea of overnight success. Wherever there's a story of a seemingly instant break-through, there's also an untold story of years of preparation. We see a person's sudden onstage appearance and think, *Well, they just got lucky. The stars aligned. They knew someone. They were in the right place at the right time.* While sometimes that can be true, there's always another truth that cannot be denied. They've just been preparing backstage for a long time.

Consider the Japanese bamboo tree. After the seed of a Japanese bamboo tree is planted, it can be watered and nurtured for years without showing any outward signs of growth. But after five years something amazing happens. After five years, the bamboo tree grows nearly ninety feet in just six weeks.[10] But the real question to consider is this: Did the bamboo tree grow in six weeks or five years?

Your growth cannot always be measured with results. If you are going to display present courage, you must settle in for the journey ahead. For now, measure your actions not your results. There will come a time when you can measure your results. But without consistent action before that, your seed will die. Your message will die with you. Instead of focusing on what you lack, focus on what you can do. Instead of focusing on results, focus on taking action.

## Why You Should Become a Farmer

So what's the answer? It's simple. Become a farmer. Farmers don't focus on results, they focus on action. Sure, the ultimate goal of a farmer is a bountiful harvest. But they know many days of action eventually lead to results.

Imagine a farmer who spends an entire day planting seed in his field. The next day he wakes up and hurries to the window, hoping to see a knee-high crop. But when he sees nothing he exclaims, "See, I knew this wasn't going to work!"

As absurd as that sounds, we do the same thing every day. We take a little bit of action, hoping for an immediate result. When we don't see results, we convince ourselves of all the reasons why our efforts will never work. Most people plant in the spring only to give up before the harvest in the fall. Don't let that be said of you. Become a farmer. Give yourself permission to measure your actions and not your results for a season.

Remember Andrew Clemens? If you ever happen to visit the State Historical Society of Iowa, you'll find one of Andrew's most famous sand art bottles on display. This famed bottle depicts George Washington, America's first president, on horseback all made by colored grains of sand.

According to the historical society, it took Clemens over eighteen months to complete this project, and it was a gift to his mother.[11] Andrew Clemens didn't make sand art just because it was profitable. He made sand art because he loved his work.

You can too. Next, let's explore together how we can build a life and work we love.

# 3

# The Secret to Building a Business and Life You Love

Across the street from where I live is a cul-de-sac. I've sat in my front yard numerous times over the years watching my kids ride bikes in that cul-de-sac. They first began riding in the cul-de-sac when my daughter, Kayla, was six and my son, Jordan, was four. He still had training wheels at the time, but he worked hard to keep up with his older sister. Around and around they went—laughing and chasing one another.

When we're kids, it's fun to ride around in circles. But what if you saw an adult riding his bike alone in a cul-de-sac continuously? Strange, right? Riding a bike in the cul-de-sac takes lots of effort but yields little progress.

## The Creative Cul-de-sac

Back in late 2010 I was tired. Between working a full-time job, raising a young family, and trying to start a business on the side, life was busy. My typical day would begin at five o'clock in the morning. After spending two hours on my passionate side-hustle business, I would commute to my day job. Often after work I would burst through the front door of our house in a hurry to get the kids to Little League practice. The weekends didn't get any less busy. Looking back, it felt quite a bit like riding my bike around and around a cul-de-sac. Can you relate?

One day I walked over to the whiteboard hanging in my home office, pulled out a marker, and wrote, "What am I ultimately trying to accomplish with all this work?" It's easy to get lost in the day-to-day grind of working, creating, and contributing. Seldom do we stop and ask, *Why are we doing all of this work in the first place? What are we hoping to accomplish with our work beyond providing for the needs of our family?*

At the time, I was a dreamer without a compass. More than anything, I needed a few guiding principles to help me weed out the opportunities that ultimately wouldn't serve me well. Up to that point I had been living by superficial principles: I wanted to pay the bills, and I wanted to work from home. But just saying "I want to work from home" is not enough. I know freelancers who traded one boss for fifty bosses because they took on fifty clients. They're always on the phone. Yes, they're working from home, but they're more stressed now than when they were working a regular day job. At the time, I was too. I needed a way to make sense of the competing demands and to figure out which opportunities and tasks were the ones that deserved my limited time.

## The Only Question That Matters

Thankfully, I found the answer I was looking for, and I'm going to share it with you. I want to walk you through the personal steps

I took to discover the things that matter most to me so that you can discover what matters most to *you*. You must decide this first before you build that dream business of yours. To find your guiding principles, you must ask yourself the only question that really matters:

> ## What am I ultimately trying to accomplish with my work?

The same day I wrote that on my whiteboard, I sat down and started writing out all the things I wanted to get out of my professional work. Out of that list came four guiding statements that I have used to help guide my work decisions ever since. Together they form the acronym "LIFE." Each letter represents a powerful guiding principle that has led me to the success I experience today. Without these four principles, I would have fallen off the path to the success I desired. LIFE stands for four values and desires, each of which can be summed up in a word or two:

- Lifestyle
- Impact
- Financial freedom
- Effort

Once I had these four success guideposts in place, I finally had complete confidence in the type of business I should build. I didn't know what my future business would be yet, but I knew where I wanted my business to take me. I knew my destination. Like me, before you even begin to define your message, you must determine the destination first. Let's look at each of these four guiding principles in detail.

### Lifestyle—I want to control the when and where of my work.

"L" stands for *lifestyle*. What kind of lifestyle do you want? I knew that I wanted to be location-independent, so I wrote down "I want to control the when and where of my work." Over the years I've discovered that my personality is one that needs lots of variety. Too much routine boxes in my creative freedom. I need that variety. Maybe you are wired that way too. Let me further break down what I mean.

#### WHEN I WORK

Time isn't a thing I can control. The days and hours pass regardless of what I do or how much work I have to get done. What I can control is when I work and for how long. There are three specific areas over which I have control when I work.

- Flexible workday hours—If I want to spend the morning going to breakfast with my wife, I'd like to be able to do that. With flexible workday hours, I can. I can choose to start work later in the day. Or when my kids come home from school, I can stop working and spend time with them. Find out how their day went and even shoot some basketball in the backyard.

- Hours worked per week—Who says I have to work until five o'clock every day? If I accomplish all my major tasks for the day, why not end the workday at noon? It's my life, and I have the power to choose.

- Unlimited vacation days—I want to determine my number of vacation days each year. Why not take a few extra days off during the summer? How about adding more vacation time around the holidays? Designing my own life empowers me to be creative and set up life according to what's most important to me.

You might read the list above and think, *That's an impossible list of benefits to achieve.* I'll admit, when I first wrote it down, it felt impossible to me too. I was so far away from any of those benefits becoming a reality in my life. My business was still a side hustle then. But writing down what I ultimately wanted helped to both ground and empower me. It helped me to stay focused on building a business that supported the personal values I had for my family and me. Every year, I average 180 days off from work. This includes weekends, traveling, my sabbatical, and family time. For the past three years I've taken a thirty-day sabbatical away from my business every July. It's a priority for me because I'm more than just a business owner. I'm also a husband, father, and friend. Kids grow up fast, and I don't want to miss out on their childhood. I also find that the time I spend away from my work makes me a better, more productive person. I come back recharged and focused. Time away from work is a value I hold dear.

Maybe your goal is not to take an entire month off from work. But know this: what you want is possible once you get clear on what's most important to you.

### WHERE I WORK

Another thing I knew was that I wanted to run a location-independent business. To be able to work from Starbucks or Panera Bread if I felt like it. To travel when the opportunity arose and to work remotely from anywhere. I wanted my office to be anyplace I could get Wi-Fi access. Having the freedom to work from anywhere was one of my ultimate goals, and I've achieved it. I know that my creativity unlocks when my location is flexible. Maybe yours does too.

### *Impact—I want to impact millions in areas that matter.*

The letter "I" in the LIFE acronym stands for *impact*. I want to impact millions in areas that matter. Like you, I want my work to make a difference. Many of us want our work to result in more than just the survival of our families. We want it to mean something in the larger world. Zig Ziglar taught that there are four levels of human progress: survival, stability, success, and significance.[1] According to Ziglar, the main reason we work is to put food on the table and take care of our families. There is nothing wrong with working for survival, but why stop there?

Once survival is achieved, we work to provide stability. Stability allows us to breathe a little and stop living paycheck to paycheck. In a recent study, one of the largest online employment websites, CareerBuilder, found that 78 percent of US workers are living paycheck to paycheck.[2] The majority of US workers are living at the survival level while striving to reach stability. No wonder so many of us are having a difficult time finding meaning and satisfaction with our work. According to data from a Gallup poll, 68 percent of US employees are disengaged at work.[3] Simply put, they are uninspired and don't see how their work makes much of a difference.

The good news is that there is another level. It is possible to gain more freedom while still making a more significant impact with your work. The top two levels of performance Zig Ziglar identifies are success and significance. Many of us would consider ourselves to be successful once we've risen above the level of stability in our work. But what I love about Ziglar's hierarchy is that the end goal is not just success. How many successful people do we know who are unhappy and unfulfilled? Significance, the next and final level, brings us to a whole new place of meaning. Don't misunderstand. Significance is not the same as making a name for ourselves and being successful in the eyes of others. True significance is about making a difference and building something that lasts. It's about focusing your work on impacting millions in areas that matter.

*Financial Freedom—I want to work on opportunities that provide unlimited income potential.*

The letter "F" in my LIFE acronym stands for *financial freedom*. We live in a world where the majority of people are living paycheck to paycheck. Many of us don't know a life outside of financing debt. But there is another way. Most people work a regular day job. Maybe you do too. There is nothing wrong with that. But under such a paradigm, the only way to get more money is through a year-end or performance bonus or a tax rebate check. With a message-based business, on the other hand, you have the opportunity to build unlimited income potential.

A few years ago my ten-year-old son, Jordan, was facing the prospect of surgery. An unusual lump had appeared on his neck. It was a stressful time for our family. After many tests and doctor visits, we came to discover it was a swollen, noncancerous lymph node. While we were certainly relieved, surgery was still required to remove it. We have health insurance, but even with health insurance, surgery is still expensive. We had to come up with a few thousand dollars to move things forward. Where was I going to come up with that money? I sat down with my wife and said, "Here's what I'm going to do. I don't know if it's going to work, but I'm going to have a forty-eight-hour spring sale. I'm going to discount some of my online courses for two days and put that info out there to my audience. The goal will be to create enough income to pay for the surgery."

I put together a page on my site with the discount codes. I sent out two emails, one announcing the forty-eight-hour sale and a second the next day, informing people there were only twenty-four hours left. We were able to generate enough extra income to make the surgery happen. The surgery was a success, and today Jordan is a healthy teenager. I'm thankful I decided to pursue a message-based business. If my income had been limited by the number of hours I could work, I never would have been able to raise the money that quickly. But because I run a message-based business, my earning potential isn't limited in the same way. Running a message-based business allows me to have unlimited income potential. That's better for my family, and it's better for me.

### Effort—I want to live up to my full potential.

The letter "E" in my LIFE acronym stands for *effort*. I'm passionate about a lot of things, but among the most important ones is this: I want to live up to my full potential. I want to be able to push myself constantly. I want to grow and to stretch my skills, and I know you do too. When you pursue your own message-based business, all that becomes possible because you're in charge of you. How much you grow depends on how much you're willing to stretch yourself. You're no longer waiting for someone to give you permission. *You* decide if you want to stand onstage and become a speaker. *You* choose if you want to become an author and move forward with writing that book.

So many of us are coasting in our work or, even worse, we're pacing ourselves, trying to save ourselves from burning out. We figure if we have to work until five o'clock, we may as well save our energy throughout the day. But when you pursue your own message-based business, you no longer need to pace yourself. You are not on clock time; you're on project time. Project time is entirely different. You jump into your work, and you work on it because you love it. You get to decide when to quit working for the day. You can take off when you want. You don't have to work until five or six o'clock or later each day.

Are you tired of feeling like you need to pace yourself in your work and life? You don't have to. You can pursue your passion with vigor and excitement. You can wake up in the morning excited about your work. Find something you're genuinely passionate about and spend your day sharing that passion.

Lifestyle. Impact. Financial freedom. Effort. *LIFE*. These four guiding principles have helped me determine what I want the end goal of all my work to be.

I encourage you to develop your own acronym that will become your guiding compass. It will serve as a guide to help you know what kind of business you should build. Like a compass, your acronym will point you toward true north. It will serve as motivation for you during times of challenge and difficulty.

This is a fun project that can perhaps help you identify some statements that can serve as guideposts as you make your way forward to creating a message-based business. It may even lead you to creating a memorable acronym that can help change your life. Either way, I can promise you this: If you take the steps in the following exercise, you'll find greater clarity. You'll be better prepared to figure out which opportunities you want to seize. You'll practice valuing the long-term over the short-term.

And you'll reach your destination much faster.

Ready to create your own acronym? Don't worry. I'll help you. You may not get it perfect the first time, but it's important to start somewhere. If you don't want to try or feel unsure about your result, you're welcome to use my LIFE acronym. But it's so empowering to be creative and design your own, I encourage you to try. Check out the following exercise for the steps to take.

# The Messenger Roadmap

My goal for you is to transform the information in this book into a personalized action plan for you. In the appendix, you'll find the Messenger Roadmap. It's a one-page plan that you'll be filling out as we work through the book together. I'll be sharing exercises along the way that will assist you in designing your message-based business.

Let's get started on the first exercise.

### EXERCISE 1

### *Your Acronym*

*Step 1. Write everything out.* Get out a blank piece of paper. Set a timer for three minutes. Ask yourself the question, *What do I want to ultimately accomplish from my work?* Write down whatever comes to mind.

If you get stuck, use the "5 Whys" exercise. Sakichi Toyoda, inventor and founder of Toyota Industries, developed a technique called the "5 Whys" as a problem-solving exercise.[4] The goal of the exercise is to drill down to the root cause of something by asking "Why?" five times. A simple adaptation is, after you find an answer for the first question, then ask, "Why is that important?" Record your new answer. While looking at what you just wrote, ask the question again. Do this five times to get at what really matters most for you.

*Step 2. Look for the excitement factor.* Once you've completed step 1, look back over your list and place a star beside the statements that excite you, the ones that resonate with you on a deep level.

*Step 3. Synthesize your list down to three to seven items.* You may find that the items you have written down overlap in various ways. Narrow your list down to a handful of items by grouping similar ones together.

*Step 4. Wordsmith your principles into a memorable acronym.* Get creative here. What are some short to midsize words that resonate with you? Make a long list and see which ones rise to the top in your mind. For me it is the word *life* that has a deeper meaning. It's a word that reminds me to bring the joy into my days, weeks, and months. It reminds me to live my life to the fullest with no regrets. I encourage you to find a word that means something to you personally. Use a thesaurus and find synonyms that will help you to fit your beliefs into an acronym. Once you choose a word, see if you can match up each letter with one of the words you've used to represent your three to seven items from step 3. Make it fun and make it memorable.

The goal of this exercise is for you to walk away with an acronym that helps you remember your big *why*. Your *why acronym*, as we call it, will serve as your compass as you build your business. Also, if my LIFE acronym resonated with you, feel free to use it for yourself. Either way, once you're done, add your acronym to the Messenger Roadmap in the appendix.

# 4

# Why You Should Build a Business Sharing Your Advice

At the age of seventeen Chandler knew that he wanted to run his own business. One day his dad handed him a book called *Rich Dad, Poor Dad*, by Robert Kiyosaki. In the book, Kiyosaki laid out why being an employee is riskier than owning your own business. Chandler loved the idea of creating a passive income, but there was one huge problem. The author's recommendation for how to build recurring income was through real estate investing. Chandler doubted that anyone would give a seventeen-year-old money to buy a duplex. The only thing he did know for sure was that he wanted to run his own business.

After graduating from high school, Chandler enrolled in the College of Charleston to learn how to run a business. But it wasn't long before he realized that none of the professors who were teaching him how to run a business had ever run a business. That's when he decided to take matters into his own hands. After some initial research online, he came across the idea of publishing his own book on Amazon. Chandler liked the fact that it was free to list his book for sale and he could earn ongoing monthly royalties from sales of his books. This opportunity had both a low barrier to entry and a passive income model.

## From College Dropout to the Inc. 5000 List

Today, Chandler Bolt is the founder of Self-Publishing School. His company has made the Inc. 5000 list two years in a row as one of America's fastest-growing private companies. But there's no denying his success story took an unlikely path. Here's how Chandler described his journey:

> My success story began when I dropped out of college. I was a C-minus English student and a bad writer, but I knew there was a story inside me. I finished that [first] book in the month between dropping out and going on vacation. Two years later, I'd publish six bestselling books. All while helping non-writers in dozens of fields publish their own bestselling books. I even built a million-dollar-plus business during that time—and I still had the free time to see family, travel to my brother's concerts and go skiing.[1]

Chandler Bolt went from college dropout to the owner of a multimillion-dollar business in just a few short years. And he did it by identifying the message he had to offer and then sharing it with the world. When you think about it, building a business by sharing your advice has several advantages to it.

## Nine Reasons to Build a Business Sharing Your Advice

Whether you realize it or not, you're probably already giving out advice for free. What if you could get paid to share what you know? What if you could earn money to teach what you are passionate about?

There is gold hidden in your life's story, the skills you've acquired, and the experiences you've gained. We're using the word *advice* in this chapter because it's a concept that is easy to understand. You may not know what your message is just yet, but I will help you uncover that in a future chapter. For now, just know people *will* pay you for your advice. I've discovered nine key benefits to building a business that's based on sharing my advice with others. See if these sound appealing to you.

1. Direct Impact—See and feel the impact your work is making.
2. Portable Lifestyle Business—Work from anywhere at any time with anyone.
3. Value-Driven Business—Get paid for value delivered, not time invested.
4. High Profit Margins—Charge what you're worth while having low overhead expenses.
5. Ability to Scale—Stop trading time for dollars and buy time instead.
6. Easy to Manage—Work with virtual employees or a small team.
7. Utilize Your Creativity—Fully embrace your creative energy.
8. Passion-Based Mission—The basis for your work is your message, passion, and purpose.
9. Unlimited Income Potential—The sky is the limit on revenue, with no salary cap.

A list of potential benefits could go well beyond the nine I've listed above. But these nine benefits represent the top reasons why

I'm so passionate about helping others. You, too, can get paid well for sharing your advice while making a significant impact. Let's look in more detail at each of these compelling reasons why you might want to do just that.

### 1. Direct Impact—See and feel the impact your work is making.

As mentioned earlier, in a past career I spent time working as an executive recruiter. One of my weekly goals was to interview ten candidates who were looking to make a job change. What I discovered surprised me. One of the main reasons people wanted to make a job change was not a lack of benefits or a low salary. It was a lack of impact. Over and over, people told me that they felt like a cog in a machine. A small fish in a big pond. Each day they would work hard on a project, then pass it along to a boss, only to find themselves wondering later if their work was making any impact at all.

But with a message-based business, you see for yourself the direct impact you are making. You can witness the value of your life's work and message in the lives of others. You work each day to create products that lead to transformation for your customers. You can ditch the cubicle and start making an impact.

### 2. Portable Lifestyle Business—Work from anywhere at any time with anyone.

A message-based business also gives you the opportunity to be location-independent. You can work from anywhere you want. You no longer have to clock in for the day. No boss is tapping his watch because you are late. There is no morning rush or zombie-like commute to work. You awake with joy each morning with the power to choose how you will spend your day. You get to decide where you will work, what you will work on, and who you will work with. A message-based business allows you to work from anywhere there's a

Wi-Fi signal. You can work from anywhere at any time with anyone. And that means total freedom and flexibility for you.

### 3. Value-Driven Business—Get paid for value delivered, not time invested.

Most people get paid for their time, which can be a problem when you desire more. Your only options are to get a second job or find a better one that pays more. A message-based business, however, is not about the number of hours you work but about the value you bring to the hours. The thing that drives your business should be the contribution you deliver to your client, not the hours you clock.

In the late 1800s Charles Steinmetz was an electrical engineer who was well known for solving complex engineering problems. At the time, a major manufacturer was struggling to locate a malfunction in one of their electrical generators. None of their employees had been able to identify the problem, so Steinmetz was called in to see what he could figure out. After arriving at the plant, Steinmetz asked to be left alone. His only requests were a notebook and a cot. He spent two entire days listening to the generator and writing down notes in his notebook. At the end of the second day, he requested a ladder and then did something unusual. He climbed the ladder, pulled out a piece of chalk, and marked an X on the side of the generator. The manufacturer's employees disassembled the machine and to their amazement found the problem exactly where the chalk mark was located.

A few weeks later, a bill arrived from Steinmetz for ten thousand dollars. The owner, who was none other than Henry Ford, protested the amount and asked for the bill to be itemized. Steinmetz sent back an itemized bill that read

Making a chalk mark $1
Knowing where to place it $9,999

Henry Ford paid the bill. Charles Steinmetz lived by a personal creed. Get paid for the value you deliver, not the time you invested.[2] Building a business based on sharing your advice is a value-driven business model. It allows you, like Charles Steinmetz, to get paid not for the time you put in but for the value inherent in what you know. Now, you might be wondering if you're even capable of bringing the kind of value that allows you to get paid well. No worries. In the pages ahead, we'll create the roadmap for you.

### 4. High Profit Margins—Charge what you're worth while having low overhead expenses.

People frequently resist starting a business because they worry about issues like overhead. Who has the money to invest in things like inventory and rent when they're just starting out? I know I worried about these things. Until I realized I didn't have to.

A message-based business has high profit margins. While most businesses squeeze out a 35 percent profit margin, you'll be enjoying 90 percent margins. Most small businesses today have to watch out for issues like hard costs and wasted materials. With a message-based business, you can be in business for less than one hundred dollars a month. Let's say you want to open a restaurant or retail store. To help you avoid making mistakes, you decide to buy into a franchise. The franchise fee sets you back several thousand dollars up front. And that's just to purchase access to the proven system. After that, you need to lease a piece of real estate.

In some cases, you'll need to purchase the initial inventory. Finally, you'll need to hire some employees. All of this before the first dollar walks into the door of your business. With this model, it could take years before you bring in a profit. But with a message-based business, you can realize a profit on your first transaction. It's a great feeling when you have a business not burdened by too many expenses.

### 5. Ability to Scale—Stop trading time for dollars and buy time instead.

Working less while making more is the ultimate dream for any business owner. In the business world this is known as leverage. What do I mean by leverage? Instead of trading your time for dollars, you trade it for more time. For me, money is important not because it buys things but because it buys time. Money buys time for me to spend with family making memories. Money buys time for me to help others in need. Money buys time for me to work on new projects that can lead to my making an even more significant contribution in the world. It's also important for me to be available to do whatever God wants me to do, and money buys time for this. Maybe there's a spiritual component for you too. For most people, though, work time weighs heavy on their hands. They're trading their time for dollars. They tap their watches. They listen to the ticking of the second hand on the clock. They can't wait to punch out so they can live their lives. But what if your life could be best lived while doing your work? What if your work could lead to more freedom?

I created my first online course in 2010. It was a course I called Job Search Mastermind, and it was designed to help job seekers find better jobs. I priced the course at ninety-seven dollars. Once I had finished creating the course, all I had to do was market it. I put it up for sale on my website. Every week after that, new sales trickled in. At the time, I was still working a day job. What was most rewarding was to come home to discover I had made money from my course while I was still working my day job. What made it even better was the sale of the course didn't require any additional time from me. I had already packaged my knowledge and expertise. Now the course was doing the work for me. This is a phenomenon that *New York Times* bestselling author Dan Miller calls SWISS Dollars—Sales While I Sleep Soundly.[3] A message-based business gives you the ability to experience both freedom and profit. I don't know about you, but I prefer to have both.

### 6. Easy to Manage—Work with virtual employees or a small team.

A message-based business is easy to manage. It doesn't require a large support staff or employee overhead. In fact in the beginning, I was the only employee of my business. It wasn't until my business began to grow that I saw a need to get some help. Even then, I started small. I hired my first virtual help for just five hours per week. My new hire handled all of the customer service emails that were coming in at the time. This freed me up and gave me back five additional hours per week to work on other things in my business.

My next hire was a graphic designer. I also hired her for just a few hours per week. She designed my weekly blog post image, logos for my online courses, and even professional-looking PDFs. Not only did this save me time from having to design my own stuff, but my designer produced a better quality of work than I ever could on my own. These two part-time hires are all I used to build my message-based business to six figures per year. Even though our business revenues have grown well beyond that over the years, I still operate my business today with fewer than fifteen virtual employees. A message-based business doesn't require a large team.

### 7. Utilize Your Creativity—Fully embrace your creative energy.

Most people see work as a necessary evil because work doesn't tap into their creativity. They are not free to be creative. With a message-based business, on the other hand, you can embrace your creativity fully. Let me share with you an example.

In my business, Wednesdays are known as "no appointment days" for me. In fact, it's rare for me to have even one item on my calendar. I work hard to protect my Wednesdays. Why? I want one entire day a week to fully express my creative energy. My home office is upstairs facing my backyard. In my backyard, we have a pond and some woods. On Wednesdays, I start my workday with a cup of coffee and my laptop. I open the windows of my office and feel the fresh morning air pouring into the room. With my laptop and coffee, I begin to write. I'm fully inspired. I'm free to be creative from any demands. With a message-based business, you can have this kind of creative freedom too.

You have 100 percent control when it comes to designing and directing your business. You're 100 percent in charge. As bestselling author Jon Acuff says in his book *Start*, "Joy is an incredible alarm clock."[4] Instead of hitting the snooze button five times and dreading Mondays, you can wake up energized and excited about your day. When you launch a business that taps into your creativity, you can't wait to wake up and start your day.

### 8. Passion-Based Mission—The basis for your work is your message, passion, and purpose.

When you think about it, a message-based business is one of the most energetic and passionate businesses to start. The reason this is true is because this type of business is built on you finding and sharing your voice with the world. Not only that, but when you combine teaching and transformation, you have a recipe for a passion-based business. I'll never forget the first webinar I hosted online. If you're unfamiliar, a webinar is similar to a seminar but it is conducted over the internet. The teacher, or facilitator, has a slide presentation, and the attendees can view the training from anywhere there's an internet connection.

For my very first webinar, I was able to get nine registrants, but only four showed up live. But I taught those four attendees as if there were hundreds on the webinar. I brought the energy and excitement for my topic that day. Where was all that energy coming from? I was passionate about teaching and I was passionate about helping others. A message-based business is exciting because it's passion-based.

### 9. Unlimited Income Potential—The sky is the limit on revenue, with no salary cap.

Acquiring wealth is a mental roadblock for many people. I know it was for me. I used to think getting rich meant that someone had to take advantage of someone else. That there were only so many pieces to the pie. When someone won (made money), that meant someone else had lost out.

But that's not how wealth works at all. Wealth is infinite. It is ever-expanding. Other people may have trouble reconciling the concept of "serving" with "making money." *Can you really do both*, they wonder, *and keep your integrity?*

The answer is yes! I was able to overcome the self-limiting belief of acquiring wealth by changing my focus. Instead of focusing on making money, I focus on making an impact. What you'll find is the two aren't unrelated. The more impact you make, the more your income will grow. Income always follows impact.

To get the first draft of this book written, I took an entire month off away from my business. I called it my "writing sabbatical." What allowed me to take a whole month off to write a book? The monthly recurring income I was already generating in my business. How did I create enough revenue to take an entire month off? I used my teaching and creativity to make a big enough impact. What am I doing with my time away from my business? Working on a book that will allow me to make an even more significant impact. It's the cycle of wealth available to those of us in a message-based business. There's unlimited income potential available to me because I work in this business, and it's available to you too. All you have to do is go after it.

These are just nine reasons why a message-based business is the way to go. You may be able to think of even more. The point is, it's worth it.

Now that you better understand the benefits of starting a message-based business, I want to give you a tool to help you fully embrace this truth. It's a short manifesto I originally created for myself. Every morning before I start my day, I read over the manifesto. It has become a daily prayer that gives me courage and purpose for my day. I call it the *Messenger Manifesto*.

# 5

# The Messenger Manifesto

Before people buy what you are selling, you must believe in your message. The two things always happen in that order. The belief has to be real: you can't fake your way to success. And it has to begin with you. You must champion your message before others will believe it. I know this from personal experience.

I remember a particular day seven years ago that left me restless. I was frustrated. I had just spent an entire workweek being nonproductive, indecisive, and unmotivated. I was in a rut. Lost in a sea of activities. Every task seemed futile, and I was on the verge of burnout. *If I love my work, why does it suddenly feel so difficult?* I wondered. According to author Michael Hyatt, his wife, Gail Hyatt, says, "People lose their way when they lose their why."[1] I certainly had lost mine. I desperately needed to reconnect with my why.

It's easy to lose sight of your why in the midst of your day-to-day tasks. Back in chapter 3, you created an acronym to help you design your work around the life you want to live. That will give you motivation for your work. But what gives us motivation *in* our work? What can help us to see our goals and projects through to completion?

Many of us begin tackling our goals and projects with enthusiasm. At first we are energized and motivated to get things done. Then once the enthusiasm wanes, the real work begins. It's what we do when we're in the valley that matters. So that day, I did the only thing I knew to do. I took out a piece of paper and wrote out my thoughts. I wrote out my why. Instead of focusing on completing tasks and projects, I desperately needed to connect with why I was doing all of this work in the first place.

Not only that, but I wanted to be reminded of my why *before* I got too far into my workday. What I wrote that day has become a manifesto I read to myself daily. Doing so reconnects me with my why. It helps me overcome my fears and points me toward my purpose. Here's what I wrote:

As I begin my day, I will choose to work from a place of mission and not fear, service and not greed, humility and not pride. I choose today to offer hope to the discouraged, purpose to the doubting, and direction to the confused. May this be my vision as I work today to build the business.

I wrote this manifesto to remind myself that how I live my message matters just as much as the things I accomplish with it. I wanted a daily reminder of what was at stake. It's not just about checking items off a to-do list. It's about living each day with mission. It's about bringing my best self to my work because my work matters.

The same is true for you. In this chapter, I'll offer you a few tools to help you approach your work with passion. Let's start by dissecting the Messenger Manifesto one phrase at a time.

## Focus on Mission, Not Fear

In 2008, Natalie had what most would consider the dream life. She was living in London working for a prestigious company. Her work was valued, and the company showed this by giving her promotions, raises, and bonuses. But inside, she was miserable. She despised the nine-to-five grind and the daily commute to work. Being more of a free spirit, she struggled with the routine of corporate life. Feeling desperate to regain her sense of freedom, she booked a one-way ticket to Canada. After quitting her job, Natalie packed up her life belongings into a suitcase and boarded the plane. Her mission was to go to Canada to participate in the World Championship Ultimate Frisbee Competition. Once the competition was over, her goal was to find work that offered her more freedom.

Shortly after the event, while still in Vancouver, she began attending every business networking event she could find in an attempt to find the right opportunity for her. One that fit her true motivations and values in life. Her networking paid off, and she soon became the cofounder of a new technology start-up. She also started a blog called *The Suitcase Entrepreneur* to share her insights and advice about how to run a lifestyle business from just a laptop and a mobile phone. She earned her revenue by way of offering online courses, digital products, and workshops, and by publishing her own book. Over the last few years, Natalie has had the opportunity to travel to over seventy countries all while running her business on the go.

In a 2017 television interview, Natalie was asked what had given her the strength to take such a big leap of faith. Her response: "I asked myself what's the worst that could happen? If I took a huge leap and failed, I would just have to go back into a job. But I had so much motivation to not do that, it was the thing that made me push forward."[2] Natalie's mission was to support other entrepreneurs while building a freedom lifestyle for herself. Do you have a mission behind your message? Without a mission it's easy for us to lose our way.

> Mission produces a singular focus;
> fear produces a scattered mind.

Former palliative care worker Bronnie Ware spent her career caring for people in the final stages of their life. Many of the patients she tended to were elderly. They often reflected on their lives during their time with Bronnie, which led her to have deep conversations with them about life. These frank conversations led Bronnie to write a memoir entitled *The Top Five Regrets of the Dying*. In her book, Bronnie outlines the top five most common regrets she heard from people at the end of their life. These top five regrets are,

1. I wish I'd had the courage to live a life true to myself, not the life others expected of me.
2. I wish I hadn't worked so hard.
3. I wish I'd had the courage to express my feelings.
4. I wish I had stayed in touch with my friends.
5. I wish that I had let myself be happier.[3]

Read back over that list. How many of those regrets would you say are connected to a feeling of fear? I could argue that four of the five regrets stem from living a fear-centered life and not a mission-centered life. The way out for us is to focus on mission, not fear.

Living on mission leads us toward action. We are no longer passive observers of our lives, but we are active participants. Fear paralyzes; mission clarifies. Living in fear and living on mission are polar opposites. You can't do both. It never works out well when we make our decisions out of fear. I would argue that when we get to the end of our lives, we will feel more regret for the choices we did not make than for the ones we did.


## Focus on Service, Not Greed

Milton Hershey. It's impossible to say that name without thinking about the chocolate candy bar. I remember visiting Hershey, Pennsylvania, as a ten-year-old boy. The moment my family drove into town it felt to me like a true-to-life Willy Wonka experience. The street lamps were shaped like large Hershey's Kisses. The house at the top of the hill toward the end of town was known as the Hershey Mansion. Near the line where people stood to enter the Hershey Museum there was an eight-foot-tall Hershey's chocolate milk carton. I really wanted to know if there was chocolate milk inside.

Not only had Milton Hershey discovered the secret recipe for making amazing chocolate, but he had successfully built an entire town from his wealth. In fact, he went so far as to build homes for his employees. The homes he built were some of the first homes in the United States to be supplied with electricity. By nearly every conceivable measuring stick, Milton Hershey was a success.

But have you ever heard of Henry Hershey? While Milton spent hours upon hours perfecting milk chocolate, Henry Hershey (Milton's father) took a much different approach to business. Henry had always been on the lookout for the next get-rich-quick scheme. He was an optimist, entrepreneur, and opportunist all wrapped into one.[4]

Unfortunately, while you can certainly admire Henry for being all of these things, his plans didn't work out so well. Henry spent his entire life moving from one big idea to the next without giving any of them an opportunity to succeed. Whereas Milton spent his life perfecting milk chocolate, Henry dabbled in real estate, oil prospecting, and fish farming, along with making cough drops, planting fruit trees, raising cattle, planting berries, and growing roses. While Milton placed his focus on just one thing, Henry had his hands in many things all at once. Ultimately, Milton found success by focusing on serving customers the best chocolate in the world; Henry failed at achieving wealth because he'd been focused on opportunities and not people. Milton's focus was on service; Henry's, on greed. Milton served people by delivering better chocolate; Henry served himself.

If there is one lesson we can take away from this story, it's this: if you want to build a business that matters, *focus on service, not greed*.

> Serving narrows our energy; greed
> spreads our energy thin.

We all know the power of a laser. Practical applications of lasers today include medical procedures, welding, cutting, laser printers, and barcode scanners. What we forget is the power of a laser comes from concentrated light. Through the process of optical amplification, light becomes a powerful tool. The same applies when it comes to serving. By choosing who we want to help and what problem we want to solve, our energy becomes focused. Like a laser, we begin to have more concentrated impact.

Greed, on the other hand, causes the opposite effect. At the root of greed is the fear of missing out. We're afraid we won't have enough money, or that we'll be left out, or that others won't think highly enough of us, so we try to fill up our lives with more. Instead of serving others, our focus is on personal gain. Jewish sages have a saying: *Tafasta merubah lo tafasta*—If you attempt to accomplish too much, you will end up accomplishing nothing at all.[5] Serving narrows our energy; greed spreads our energy thin. When we get clear on who we want to serve, every other decision becomes easier and more focused.

## Focus on Humility, Not Pride

Our culture has a fascination with superheroes. After all, who wouldn't want to fly like Superman, swing like Spiderman, and have superhuman strength like Wonder Woman?

But we have an equal fascination with villains. Good villains have some redeeming, likable qualities. They are persuasive and confident, and they stop at nothing to get what they want. When you think about it, they have many of the same qualities as the superheroes; they are just misdirected. The distinguishing factor is that one focuses on the humility of serving, the other focuses on pride. But there's something even better than being the hero. It's being the guide.

> Humility puts the focus on others;
> pride puts the spotlight on yourself.

Too many people these days, especially on social media, are looking to make a name for themselves. They measure their worth by the number of subscribers they have. They want to be seen as successful in the eyes of others. But trying to position oneself as the hero is exhausting. When your focus is on being the hero, you're forced to put the spotlight on yourself. There's a persona to live up to or an act to play. Only in this scenario, the show never ends. Becoming the guide is an easier and more rewarding path. The focus shifts to being helpful. When you are not the hero, you don't have to have it all together.

Whether you desire to write, speak, teach, or coach for a living, being the guide is the best way to go. But how can you become the guide? Adopt these three daily practices: offer hope to the discouraged, bring purpose to the doubting, and provide direction to the confused.

## Focus on Hope, Not Discouragement

You don't have to look far to find discouragement in our society. It abounds whatever our language, race, age, or status. As messengers, our role is to breathe hope into discouraged hearts. We do that by showing we care. As former president Theodore Roosevelt famously said, "No one cares how much you know, until they know how much you care."[6]

In the classic movie *Dead Poets Society*, Professor John Keating faces a huge undertaking—teaching a group of misfit boys how to appreciate the arts and literature. Most of Professor Keating's students see little value in learning poetry from the dead poets of the past. Most of them see little value in their own future as well. Professor Keating knows he must take drastic actions to help encourage and awaken the hearts of his students. So he begins a series of exercises to get them out of their seats and become active participants. The professor's passion for creative work begins to instill hope in the boys. "No matter what anybody tells you, words and ideas can change the world," Professor Keating tells them.[7] He wants to inspire them toward an amazing future.

> Hope inspires the future;
> discouragement dreads the past.

The professor's goal was to shift his students' focus away from the past and fix their eyes on the future instead. But this story brings up another interesting question. Who is the real hero of this story? You might argue that Professor Keating is the hero. He's the hero because he inspired a new generation of students to go after their dreams, right? Well, yes, he does inspire them. But on closer inspection, you may well conclude that the real heroes are the students. The next generation of change-makers who will go on to make a difference in the world. Movie fans love this classic because we see our own lives in the lives of the students. We too want to have meaning, purpose, and passion.

If you want to have influence on others, you must learn how to encourage the heart. You can best do that by showing empathy toward other people's challenges and demonstrating you care. People don't want you to fix them; they want you to understand them. This begins with the heart. When you encourage another person's heart, you become that person's guide. Then, once you have someone's heart, you can take them anywhere. It's by encouraging others that we move people from discouragement to hope.

## Focus on Purpose, Not Doubt

There are only a handful of movies I'll watch over and over again, and *The Karate Kid* is at the top of the list. In the opening scenes of the movie Daniel LaRusso, an only son raised by a single mother, reluctantly moves from the East Coast to the West Coast. Leaving his high school friends behind, he must start all over in a new place. Just his luck, he runs into a group of bullies determined to make his life miserable.

Then enters Mr. Miyagi. He's more than just the maintenance man for the apartment building. Mr. Miyagi has a black belt in karate. Daniel, desperate to learn karate in order to defend himself, begs Mr. Miyagi to become his teacher. After much coercion, Mr. Miyagi finally agrees. But what happens next is nothing like what Daniel expected. Instead of learning special karate techniques in the dojo, Daniel finds himself performing chores like painting the fence and waxing the car. It doesn't take long before Daniel believes he is just being taken advantage of. What he doesn't realize is that Mr. Miyagi is teaching him the fundamentals of karate. Daniel wants to learn how to do a roundhouse kick, but Mr. Miyagi is giving him core teachings first. One of my favorite lines in the movie is when Mr. Miyagi tells Daniel, "First learn stand, then learn fly."[8]

> Purpose produces confidence;
> doubt births inaction.

This is an important lesson for all of us aspiring guides. Some of the people we hope to serve want the results without the work. Like Daniel LaRusso, they want to skip over the fundamentals. Our duty as the guide is to educate them. By educating the head, we help our audience move from doubt to confidence.

## Focus on Direction, Not Confusion

Like a lot of kids who grew up in the 1980s, I wanted to be Luke Skywalker. I secretly believed a lightsaber was a real weapon. If only I could convince my parents to buy me one for Christmas! Just as Ralphie in the movie *A Christmas Story* wanted a Red Ryder BB gun, I wanted a lightsaber. (Ralphie ended up getting the BB gun even though his parents believed he'd shoot his eye out. I guess I never got the lightsaber because my parents thought I'd cut my arm off.)

The story of Luke Skywalker is timeless because it follows something called the Hero's Journey. In 1975 George Lucas had already written two drafts of Star Wars. Yet something was still missing from the story. That's when Lucas rediscovered a book he'd first read in college: Joseph Campbell's *The Hero with a Thousand Faces*.[9] In the book, Campbell points out that all stories through history are expressions of the same story pattern. The story starts with the main character's call to adventure. Before too long the character meets a mentor. The mentor is not the hero of the story. The main character is the hero. The mentor is the one who gives direction and helps the character become the hero he or she was meant to be.

> Direction calls us to adventure;
> confusion leads to delay.

This Hero's Journey blueprint led George Lucas to the single story he needed to describe the imaginary universe that was in his head. The Hero's Journey perfectly describes the relationship between Yoda and Luke Skywalker. Yoda's role as the guide is to help Luke Skywalker step into his greatness. One of my favorite lines in the movie is when Yoda says to Luke, "Do. Or do not. There is no try."[10] Yoda knows that in order for Luke to be successful, he has to move him from delay to action. We must help the people we want to serve to do the same.

## The Thirty-Day Messenger Manifesto Challenge

Trying to make your mark or make a name for yourself is exhausting. Screaming louder than everyone else in order to be heard is not the answer. While your competition is frantically trying to shout louder, each day you can quietly go about your business of serving, encouraging, and guiding. Instead of shouting louder, you can spend your day perfecting the practice of guiding and serving others. You can go about your day as Professor Keating (encouraging the heart), Mr. Miyagi (educating the head), or Yoda (empowering the hands). Life takes on meaning and our days take on purpose when we focus on being the guide, not the hero.

Did you resonate with this manifesto? Did it tap into any desires you feel deep within yourself? If so, I have a challenge for you that I hope you will accept.

Believing in your message begins by leaning into it daily. Write down the Messenger Manifesto and put it in a place where you can recite it daily. I also have a downloadable tool kit for the Messenger Manifesto that you can access for free at: YourMessageMatters Book.com/tools.

Let the Messenger Manifesto become your daily motivation to step into who you were meant to be. People out there are waiting for your dream to become reality. They need your help. Their future help depends on your present courage. But before you can begin to help, you must first define your message. Let me show you how to combine purpose, people, and passion into a business you'll love!

# The Messenger Roadmap

## *Create Your Messenger Manifesto*

It's time to complete your next exercise. As mentioned before, you'll find the Messenger Roadmap located in the appendix. If you like my version of the Messenger Manifesto and want to adopt it as your own, feel free to add it there. Here it is again:

> As I begin my day, I will choose to work from a place of mission and not fear, service and not greed, humility and not pride. I choose today to offer hope to the discouraged, purpose to the doubting, and direction to the confused. May this be my vision as I work today to build the business.

If you'd prefer to create your own manifesto, here are a few questions to answer that will help you do just that:

1. *What values do you want your business to promote?* For example, I want my business to support the values of service, humility, and living on mission. What values do you want yours to support?

2. *What would be the opposites of those values?* In the example of my business, the opposite of living on mission is living in fear. The opposite of service is greed and the opposite of humility is pride. What are the opposites of the values you want

to promote? Knowing this can help you to see the things you want to help your audience avoid.

3. *List a few* before *and* after *attributes of your ideal audience.* These are the ones I came up with for my audience: moving from discouragement to hope, from doubt to purpose, and from confusion to direction.

4. *Craft your ideas into three or four sentences.* Once you've gone through the three steps above, you're ready to construct your ideas into a powerful manifesto of your own. Don't try to get it perfect, just focus on trying to incorporate all your ideas into three or four sentences. A great way to start your manifesto is to complete this phrase: "As I begin my day, I will . . ." Go ahead and construct your first draft manifesto now.

5. *Add your manifesto to the Messenger Roadmap.* Whether you craft your own manifesto or use mine, take a moment right now and fill it in on your Messenger Roadmap in the appendix.

# PART 2

# DEFINE
# YOUR
# MESSAGE

I am the oldest of three boys, and when we were young, my brothers and I lived with our parents on a forty-five-acre campground. The camp housed seven horses, some of which seemed wild at times to us young boys.

One fall, when I was twelve years old, my brothers and I decided to venture over the fence to get a closer look at the horses. They were standing at the top of a distant hill, farther than we felt like walking, so we strategized on how we could get them to come closer.

Not having any grain with us to shake in the bucket (our usual method for getting the horses to trot over to us), we decided to shake some rocks in the bucket instead. Sure enough, all seven horses came galloping our way, but now we had a different problem. They weren't slowing down!

"Run!" I yelled. I tossed the bucket of rocks in the air and jumped over the fence to safety. But when I looked back I saw that my youngest brother was stuck in the mud. It had rained the day before, and his little shoes were now trapped in the deep grooves the horses had left in the once-sloshy soil. He was paralyzed. I still remember the fear in his eyes. I jumped back over the fence and pulled him right out of his shoes—just in time. As we lay in the grass on the safe side of the fence, we had no words for each other. Just the panting of our breath and the relief that none of us were hurt.

Have you ever felt stuck? Have you ever felt hopeless? Life has a way of running at us like wild horses. Whether the problems we face have to do with finances, school, work, relationships, or starting a business, we often see no way out. Like my brother feeling stuck in a helpless situation, we too feel paralyzed on the path forward.

What do you do when you have a burning desire to build a business with your message, yet you feel completely stuck? That's precisely how Fred, a customer of mine, described his situation of trying to get his business up and running: "It feels like I'm stuck in a tar pit while wondering if my strength, passion, and intrinsic motivation are enough to carry me through. Then when I do finally ask for help, I'm thrown a rope that leads to more rope and more rope."

A lack of clarity shuts down any hope of progress. Trying to get clear becomes a daily mental battle. Hopeless feelings lead to negative thought patterns, and negative thinking leads to inaction with no hope of how to get out of the pit.

When we're stuck, we usually think it's because we have no options. But a lack of options is not why we are stuck. Having *too many choices* is why we are stuck. We live in a different world than the one that existed a hundred years ago. That can work to your advantage. There are a million ways to make a million dollars today; you just need to choose one.

The good news is that there is a remedy for the *too many choices* situation. The answer is found in the act of defining your message. You're not stuck because you're immobile. You're stuck because you're unsure of the next step. That's what we're going to help you figure out. You'll be able to choose your next step once you've identified your message.

The path to clarity lies in defining your message. Many of us lack clarity because we have yet to answer three important questions that relate to three important areas:

1. Purpose: What is your unique gift?
2. People: Who do you want to help?
3. Passion: What problem will you solve?

In part 2 we will walk through several exercises that will help you nail down three critical areas of your business: your purpose, the people you will serve, and the passion you'll pursue (also known as the problem your work will address). Over the years I've found that the act of confirming all three areas ignites a spark in those who want to start a message-based business.

Let's get to work. It's time to identify your life's message.

# 6

# The Ignite Your Message Framework

Fire is essential to survival. Just watch a season of the long-running TV show *Survivor*. Each season a new set of contestants test their creativity by trying to ignite a fire with little to no resources. In the first fourteen seasons of the American version of *Survivor*, not one contestant had been able to start a fire using only natural resources. Finally on *Survivor South Africa: Malaysia*, Hein Vosloo, who'd lived in the African bush for more than twenty years, boasted that he knew seven different methods for igniting a fire. Using just ropes and sticks, Hein became the first contestant in *Survivor* history to start a fire without using flint, a lighter, or matches.[1]

Clearly there are many ways to ignite a fire. But whatever creative approach is used, three elements must exist for fire to be created—heat, fuel, and oxygen. The absence of any one of these elements will make the attempt futile. Similarly, if you want to build a message-based business, you also need to have three elements in place. Those three essential elements are as important as heat, fuel, and oxygen.

6.1

## Ignite Your Message

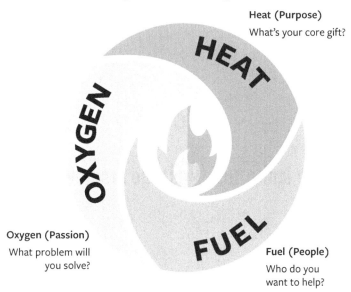

Heat (Purpose)
What's your core gift?

Oxygen (Passion)
What problem will
you solve?

Fuel (People)
Who do you
want to help?

*Heat represents your purpose.* Your purpose is found in your unique gift (how you show up best in this world). Finding your purpose is not an external pursuit, but an inward journey. You don't *find* your purpose in life; you uncover it. It's buried deep within.

It works like a geothermal heat pump. Scientists are now utilizing a secret our cave ancestors knew long ago. Regardless of how cold it is outside, if you go far enough into a cave, you'll find a consistent fifty-degree temperature. Like solar panels bring cost-effective electricity to your home, geothermal heat pumps can keep your home warm by burying the pipes deep into the ground.[2] Uncovering the heat or purpose of your life works the same way. It's an inward journey, not an external process.

*Fuel represents the people you want to serve.* There is no fire without fuel just like there is no business without people. Your purpose and your passion only become useful when applied to serving a specific group of people. Who needs to hear your message? Who desperately needs the solutions and advice you have to offer? Who is your message *specifically* for? No, your message is not for everyone. I know you want to help everyone. But when you try to reach everyone, you end up reaching no one. If you want your message to resonate, it must be directed to help a specific group of people.

*Oxygen represents your passion.* When you pursue something you are passionate about, it breathes life into your message. Some business experts say don't pursue your passion, but instead pursue what's profitable. The problem with that philosophy is it places the emphasis in the wrong place. When work is only about collecting the Benjamins and not about serving people, our decisions become shortsighted. I want you to know it's entirely possible to pursue both. I want to help you discover the intersection between the two.

You must identify all three elements—purpose, passion, and people—in order to define your message. Many people get clear about two out of three, only to become frustrated and wonder why their business isn't growing and their influence isn't spreading. You don't have to miss by much to miss the mark. Let's look at what happens when you only get two of the three correct.

6.2

## Purpose + Passion - People = Hobby

**1 Hobby**

**Heat (Purpose)**
What's your core gift?

**Oxygen (Passion)**
What problem will
you solve?

**Fuel (People)**
Who do you
want to help?

In the above equation, we've created a hobby business by never taking the time to identify who is our audience. Who most needs my message? What group of people can I attach myself to in order to become their guide? Is there evidence in the marketplace of people spending money to solve problems related to my passion? A hobby business comes about when we are only focused on ourselves.

The equation above explains why many bloggers fail. Instead of creating blog posts that answer the big questions their audience has, their blog posts feel more like online journaling. If you want to use a blog as a marketing tool, it must serve your audience in some way. The great secret to blogging is this: your blog isn't about you at all. The same is true about your business.

6.3

## Passion + People - Purpose = Party

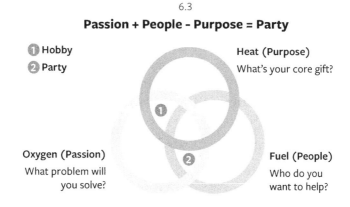

1 Hobby
2 Party

Heat (Purpose)
What's your core gift?

Oxygen (Passion)
What problem will
you solve?

Fuel (People)
Who do you
want to help?

What is your purpose? It is what you do that adds value to the lives of others. Your purpose is about identifying your strengths and fully leveraging them to create value in the world. When value is created, income and impact are the natural by-products even if they aren't the primary goal. When you have purpose, you have one of the key elements of a message-based business. When you don't . . . well, you have something else.

When you gather people around a passion alone, you have the makings of a party, not of a business model. I've spoken with many people who have amassed a large Facebook or Instagram following. Yet they struggle with how to monetize their efforts. That's because their focus was on hosting a party, not building a business. A real business solves problems for people, and the messenger solves the problem by utilizing his or her unique purpose.

6.4

## Purpose + People - Passion = Lack of Focus

1 Hobby                              Heat (Purpose)
2 Party                              What's your core gift?
3 Lack of Focus

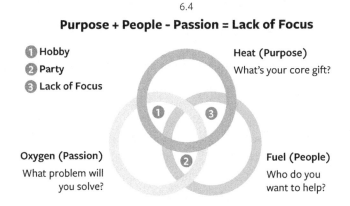

Oxygen (Passion)                     Fuel (People)
What problem will                    Who do you
you solve?                           want to help?

"I want to help everybody!" I can't tell you how many times I've heard this over the years. Most entrepreneurs fight against the idea that their message is not for everyone. They worry that if they focus on a niche in the market, it will take much longer to attract a big enough audience to sustain a business. What they fail to realize is that when you communicate to everyone, you reach no one.

Most people don't resonate with a watered-down message. When I began my first blog in 2009, I started as a career and life coach. I wanted to be a coach for everyone. It didn't matter what career a person was in or their stage of life. What were the results of my effort? You probably guessed it. I got zero traction. It wasn't until I niched down to being a career coach for accounting professionals that my business began to take off. In order for you to achieve focus in your business, you too will need three things:

1. Specific communication
2. Strategic action
3. Single market

Let's look at these more closely.

## Specific Communication—The More Specific You Can Be, the More Powerful Your Communication Becomes

A few years ago I was interviewing famed copywriter Ray Edwards. We were discussing the issue of whether or not to niche down in business when he said something that had me scrambling for a paper and pen. He said, "The more specific you can be, the more powerful your communication becomes." That's the power of finding a single passion or niche to pursue. The biggest mistake I made in the early stages of my business was having a lack of focus. Back then, I wanted my message to be for everyone. I figured that building a business was hard enough. I didn't want to make things harder by narrowing my market. Doing so would mean it would take even longer to reach my intended audience, right? Wrong.

I wish I'd been able to hear Ray's advice years before, when I was first starting out. I would have saved lots of wasted time and effort. Once I discovered the importance of niching down my audience, my communication became more powerful. Since my message hit more close to home with my ideal audience, they began to reach out to me for help. And that meant I could then help more people.

## Strategic Action—Become a Serial Entrepreneur, Not a Simultaneous Entrepreneur

There's a big difference between a serial entrepreneur and a simultaneous entrepreneur. A serial entrepreneur focuses on one thing at a time. A simultaneous entrepreneur tries to build multiple businesses all at once. One approach is driven by focus, the other by activity. You need more than just activity in order to succeed. As Michael Hyatt says, "Productivity is not about getting more things done. It's about getting the right things done."[3]

In order to say yes to the right things, we must learn to say no to everything else. At first, the practice of saying no makes you wonder what you are missing out on. But the reward of focus is progress. I'd rather move one thing ten steps forward than advance ten things one step. That's the power of focus.

About a year into my message-based business journey, I started three separate blogs, each on different topics. I convinced myself at the time that I was doing the smart thing. I wasn't putting all of my eggs in a single basket. What I failed to realize at first was just how much energy I was expending in all these different directions. But this soon became clear. What I did for one website had to be done again on all the other websites. All of the time and energy of building an email list for one business had to be done for the others. I would get to the end of my day and wonder if I'd accomplished anything meaningful. I was spinning a ton of plates but getting nowhere. It was a classic case of death by a thousand paper cuts. Little things were eating up all of my time.

The key to success, though, isn't complicated. Author Benjamin Hardy, in his book *Willpower Doesn't Work*, says, "Success isn't that difficult; it merely involves taking twenty steps in a singular direction. Most people take one step in twenty directions."[4] Success doesn't come faster if a person chooses to become a simultaneous entrepreneur. In fact, there's a very good chance it will come more slowly.

At the root of my actions was one thing: fear. I was afraid I would waste time if I focused on building one business only to discover it was the wrong one. I thought by working on three different businesses all at once I would have a greater chance of success. That belief couldn't be any further from the truth.

My biggest problem back in those early days was broken focus. I never fully devoted time to any one task or project. I dabbled. It wasn't uncommon for me to have five projects 20 percent of the way done. Once I realized my mistake, I had to make some tough choices. And I did. I stopped a popular weekly podcast I was recording at the time. I stopped publishing weekly posts on two other blogs. I instead put 100 percent of my effort into growing one business. My results multiplied as my focus narrowed. The same will be true for you.

## Single Market—Become Known for Something to Someone

*Focus sounds great*, you may think, *but I'm not sure what to focus on.* How do you overcome a lack of focus? That's easy: decide to become known for something. Maybe you have lots of interests. That's great. Still, give yourself permission for the next two to five years to become known for just one thing. You can always pivot later. I first became known as a "career coach for accounting professionals." Two years later, I pivoted and became known as "the blogging guy." Who knows what the next few years of evolution will bring in my business. Time will tell. But I had to start somewhere. And in the beginning, it's far easier to become known for something than to become known for everything.

So far, we've talked about the elements you need to have in place in order to define your message, and we've looked at what can go wrong when not all of those elements are in place. Now it's time to start defining your message. How do you start? It all goes back to answering those three simple questions:

1. Purpose: What is your unique gift?
2. People: Who do you want to help?
3. Passion: What problem will you solve?

Over the next few chapters we will do a deep dive into how you can best answer these three questions in relation to your unique situation. We will walk through some exercises and even complete an assessment to get you absolute clarity on the business you should build. So let's get started.

# 7

# Purpose

## What Is Your Unique Gift?

At the turn of the twentieth century, Texas largely depended on cattle ranching, farming, and lumber for its economy. While there were a few ranchers who struck oil, it wasn't enough to make any significant impact on the local economy. Captain Anthony Lucas, a salt dome formations expert, was convinced that Spindletop Hill, four miles south of Beaumont, Texas, had oil. Most experts disagreed with Lucas's assessment and thought he was wasting his time drilling for oil. Still, Lucas persisted. Unfortunately, after unsuccessfully drilling down to over 575 feet, Lucas ran out of money. But he never gave up on his dream.

Lucas located a few additional investors who not only helped provide capital but also brought in some drilling mud experts. After reaching a depth of over 1,139 feet, finally, on January 10, 1901, Lucas struck oil. But the story doesn't end there. The gusher of oil was so strong it shattered the wooden barracks and blew oil over 100 feet high. The "Lucas Geyser," as it is known, produced over 100,000 barrels of oil per day in its first ten days. Just a year earlier, the total annual Texas oil production was only 836,000 barrels. Captain Lucas's Spindletop geyser topped the entire state of Texas's previous year's total in just nine days. At the time, Spindletop was the largest gusher of oil in the world. This had such a significant impact that it affected the entire world.

Michel T. Halbounty, coauthor of *Spindletop: The True Story of the Oil Discovery That Changed the World* (New York: Random House, 1952), said this event changed the way people would live all over the world. "It caused the United States to become a world power. It revolutionized transportation through the automobile industry." On top of that, Texaco and Gulf Oil were formed for the purpose of the production of oil at Spindletop. All of this impact because one man decided to drill deep.[1]

Finding your purpose in life is like drilling for oil. You have genius inside you. You may not know it yet, but it's down there. You don't find your purpose in a thing, a job, a career, or an opportunity. We all know people who lost their purpose when they lost their job or career. That's because they mistakenly placed their purpose in something that can change. Your real purpose is found in what's changeless about you. It's your unique gift that's buried deep inside of you. Like Anthony Lucas with Spindletop, we have to be willing to go deep enough to uncover the riches in our depths. Are you ready to be awakened? To uncover your purpose and add value to others' lives, you must do two things:

1. Uncover your unique gift (your natural ability).
2. Apply your influencer voice (how you best show up for others).

In this chapter, we will explore two simple exercises that will help you uncover and apply your unique gift.

## Finding Your One Word

I want you to start this inward journey by finding your one word. Finding your word can awaken you to new life. It can give you meaning and purpose. Once you have your one word, you'll never doubt the value you can bring to others. Your one word will describe how you show up best, what you bring to every situation. Remember, you don't find your purpose in life, you uncover it. You need to do the hard work of digging deep and looking inward, as if you're hunting after diamonds. Which is, after all, exactly what you're doing.

Now I want to walk you through a simple two-question exercise. You will be tempted to just read over it and move on. I urge you not to do that. An essential element to building a message-based business is to uncover what's unique about you. For this exercise, you'll need the help of other people. As a friend once told me, "It's hard to read the label when you're inside the bottle." You need an outside perspective. I want you to identify five people who know you best and ask them these two questions.

*Question 1. If you could describe me using three different words, what words would you choose (example: positive, resourceful, insightful, etc.)?* The goal of this exercise is for you to collect fifteen words or more that describe you. Once you start getting responses back, begin collecting them into a document. As you compile them, look for words that are synonyms. Begin grouping similar words together. If you get the same word multiple times from different people, don't just write it down once. Write the same word multiple times. You're looking for patterns. Can you identify a single word that stands out? Is there a word given to you that especially resonates with you?

If after doing this work you find that you're still struggling with identifying a single word, then I want you to create what's known as a word cloud. A word cloud is a visual representation of a word or words commonly used in a list or document. There are many free tools online to help you create a word cloud. Just copy and paste your list of words and the word cloud will create a visual representation of the words for you. If a certain word is mentioned more than others, it will be displayed in a larger font. My wife printed out and framed my word cloud as a surprise gift for my office. It now hangs in my office as a reminder of the value I can bring to others' lives and how I show up best for others.

Some people love and connect with the words they find as a result of doing this exercise. But what if you don't like yours? Remember this quote from my friend, author Brian Dixon: "What's obvious to you is magic to other people."[2] We often don't see the value we bring to the world, even when it's pointed out to us. The things that come easily to us, we assume, are also easy for everyone else. But that's just not true. You have a gift. Your gift is needed in the world.

*Question 2. When have you seen me come fully alive, and what was I doing at the time?* This is another insightful question to ask in your purpose discovery process. The answer provides clues about the context in which you best thrive. What context are you in when you come fully alive? We all have certain environments that awaken and invigorate us.

I think of my father as an example. For over forty years he has been a teacher and basketball coach. He spent the first twenty of those years in a high school setting. The remaining twenty were spent working at a college. If you were to meet him on the street, you'd get the impression that he's a very reserved, quiet, and even introverted person. Put him on the sidelines of a basketball game, though, and he comes fully alive. He's not afraid to let the referee know he made a bad call. Even people in the stands can hear him in a time-out huddle urging his team to step up their game. He is most alive in the context of training and coaching young people.

You too have certain contexts that ignite your passion. What are you doing in such moments? Maybe you come to life in one-on-one conversations because you're great at asking clarifying questions and helping others get unstuck. Maybe you come to life when you're speaking to a group of people. Or maybe your heart flutters when you have an open calendar for the day. An entire day that allows you to express your creative work. You may already have some clues as to when you come fully alive, but it's still important to get the insights of others.

## Embrace Your One Word

When I first did this exercise years ago, the word that people in my life shared most often was *resourceful*. I hadn't thought of myself as particularly resourceful, but they had. And so, armed with this information, I began to realign my life's work by seizing those opportunities that best allowed me to be resourceful. Big changes didn't happen overnight. But things began to slowly fall into place as I leaned into my gift. I saw blogging as a way to express my resourcefulness, and so I started a blog. Then came podcasts, webinars, and membership sites, along with coaching, writing books, and hosting events. Over time I began to see my resourcefulness fully expressed in my work.

One August morning while traveling with my parents, my brothers, our wives, and all of our kids, we made a stop along the Appalachian Trail. As we were hiking, I came across a unique rock. It was smooth and stood up by itself like it belonged on a bookshelf. Too big to put in my pocket, I placed it in my backpack and we kept on hiking.

We brought the rock home to Florida. Unsure of what to do with it, I left it in the garage. A few days later, my wife showed up in my office with a surprise. She had decoupaged a word onto the rock. The word was *Resourceful*. She was one of the people I asked to describe my one word, and it was her way of encouraging me to live it out. That rock still sits on my bookshelf in my home office today. Whenever I begin to doubt my worth or question my abilities, I look over at the rock. It reminds me of the mission I've been given. It reminds me that I have an obligation to steward that gift well.

But that's not all there is to the story. Because when we were hiking along the Appalachian Trail, we also came across a number of small shiny rocks. They sparkled in the sunlight, appearing to look like gold. They were everywhere along the trail. I pulled out my cell phone to try to identify what kind of rocks they were. That's when I discovered these rocks had a name—iron pyrite, also known as fool's gold. Iron pyrite appears valuable, but it's just a shiny distraction. Fool's gold represents all of the worthless distractions that come our way when we are trying to live our purpose. Seeking after it doesn't serve our mission, it deters it. Many of us know this as the *shiny object syndrome.*

*Entrepreneur* magazine guest contributor Jayson DeMers defined shiny object syndrome this way: "At its core, shiny object syndrome (SOS) is a disease of distraction, and it affects entrepreneurs specifically because of the qualities that make them unique."[3] While we could say the drive for more is often ambition, could it also be an underlying fear of missing out? Whether we realize it or not, most of us fear either success or failure. We fear being wrong. We fear the unknown. We fear our own abilities. We fear being criticized. We fear wasting our time. It feels safer to live a life of pursuing distractions than it does to live a life on mission. But it's not. Doing more doesn't equal having more. While distractions fill up our calendars, they don't fill up our bank accounts.

So it is, my friend, that along life's journey you have a daily choice: you can serve your mission or you can serve your fear. Joy comes into your life when you see the fool's gold but choose to ignore it because you're on a mission. Your mission is to show up daily and live out your one word. But how can we lean into and live out our unique gift? We do so by combining it with our influencer voice.

## Discover Your Primary Influencer Voice

You might be wondering, *Okay, I know what my unique gift may be, but now what?* Once you uncover your unique gift (your one word), you need to make the best use of it. The best way to do that is to apply what I call your influencer voice.

Your influencer voice is how you naturally express your unique gift. Some of us best process our thinking and express our abilities in writing. Others of us best express our gift through speaking. Give us a topic to discuss and the ideas and illustrations just flow. Still others of us are great at asking insightful questions and coaching others through challenges. The point is that you have a natural way to influence others. If you're not sure what that is, we have a tool to help you discover it.

The simple assessment below will help you discover your primary influencer voice. This is by no means a definitive test, but it will give you a jump start to help you see how you best express yourself.

The following assessment is designed to provide insight as to what your strongest influencer voice may be by assessing four primary influencer voices: writer, speaker, teacher, and coach. These represent the four primary ways messengers get their message heard. The goal of this test is twofold. The first goal is to identify your primary influencer voice. Whichever one comes to the top is the best place to get started. For example, if you score the highest with "writer," then you may want to start by launching a blog. Your first income strategy may be to write a book. By leaning into your primary influencer voice, you will create flow in your business.

The second goal of the test is to determine your influencer voice order. In other words, from highest to lowest, how do you score in the four influencer voice categories? For example, my influencer voice order is teacher, writer, speaker, and coach. This was a bit of a surprise when you consider my first business was writing a "career coach" blog.

But on further inspection, you can see how I fully leveraged the influencer voices of writing and teaching. Blogging was how I expressed my writing voice. Posting a weekly blog helped me to attract my ideal audience. One of the first ways I monetized my blog was by creating a sixteen-week online course called Job Search Mastermind. I didn't realize it at the time, but I was employing my teaching influencer voice.

Now that you understand the two goals of the Influencer Voice Assessment, it's your turn. Do not overthink each statement but decide quickly and intuitively. There are no right or wrong answers. If you want an outside perspective, take the test along with someone who knows you best. For a free online version (including action steps and coaching points), go to YourMessageMatters Book.com/quiz.

Read each statement below and rate the statement as follows: 1 (Never), 2 (Rarely), 3 (Sometimes), 4 (Very Often), or 5 (Always).

## The Influencer Voice Assessment

|  | 1<br>Never | 2<br>Rarely | 3<br>Sometimes | 4<br>Very Often | 5<br>Always |
|---|---|---|---|---|---|
| 1. I am naturally drawn toward action. |  |  |  |  |  |
| 2. I enjoy helping others solve problems. |  |  |  |  |  |

| | 1<br>Never | 2<br>Rarely | 3<br>Sometimes | 4<br>Very Often | 5<br>Always |
|---|---|---|---|---|---|
| 3. I am energized by the opportunity to influence a live audience. | | | | | |
| 4. I give shape to ideas by linking them to feelings and thoughts. | | | | | |
| 5. I enjoy taking a complex subject and creating my own simple outline. | | | | | |
| 6. I prefer to work in groups and teams over working alone. | | | | | |
| 7. I am an avid reader and learner. | | | | | |
| 8. I love creating my own worksheets and tools. | | | | | |
| 9. When I plan, I see both the vision and the details of a project or goal. | | | | | |
| 10. I am a natural storyteller. | | | | | |
| 11. I work best when I can process ideas and concepts through writing first. | | | | | |
| 12. When in a group, I have a keen awareness of whether people are engaged. | | | | | |
| 13. I tend to be more at ease when teaching a larger group, rather than a small group of people. | | | | | |
| 14. When I learn something new, I tend to want to share it with others around me. | | | | | |
| 15. I don't mind being a bit vulnerable if necessary. | | | | | |
| 16. I love to connect the dots on a subject and come up with an innovative solution. | | | | | |
| 17. When it comes to completing projects, I tend to be task-driven. | | | | | |

| | 1<br>Never | 2<br>Rarely | 3<br>Sometimes | 4<br>Very Often | 5<br>Always |
|---|---|---|---|---|---|
| 18. Parties and people energize me. | | | | | |
| 19. My personality tends toward introversion, but I still have a high need to influence others. | | | | | |
| 20. I desire to be as free as possible from social demands. | | | | | |
| 21. I enjoy one-on-one and small group interaction over working in large groups. | | | | | |
| 22. I am energized by spending time reading and thinking. | | | | | |
| 23. I love to learn all I can on a topic and then create my own summary or application. | | | | | |
| 24. I prefer to influence, persuade, and motivate others in person. | | | | | |
| 25. I tend to speak the truth in love rather than staying silent in order to avoid conflict. | | | | | |
| 26. The idea of teaching a group of people every month excites me. | | | | | |
| 27. I am naturally perceptive and curious. | | | | | |
| 28. I like to use a sense of humor as a way to connect with others. | | | | | |
| 29. I am energized by the thought of hosting an hour-long webinar to a large audience. | | | | | |
| 30. I often see the hidden potential in others before they do. | | | | | |
| 31. I value creative expression and deep thinking. | | | | | |
| 32. I prefer to not be overscheduled on my calendar. | | | | | |

## Scoring the Assessment

Record the scores that you wrote down in the correct columns below. For example, if you wrote down 5 (Always) for question number one, then write "5" next to question 1 below. After writing down your scores for all thirty-two questions, add up the total for each column.

| Coach Score | Speaker Score | Writer Score | Teacher Score |
|---|---|---|---|
| 1. = _____ | 3. = _____ | 4. = _____ | 5. = _____ |
| 2. = _____ | 6. = _____ | 7. = _____ | 8. = _____ |
| 9. = _____ | 10. = _____ | 11. = _____ | 13. = _____ |
| 17. = _____ | 12. = _____ | 16. = _____ | 14. = _____ |
| 21. = _____ | 15. = _____ | 20. = _____ | 19. = _____ |
| 25. = _____ | 18. = _____ | 22. = _____ | 23. = _____ |
| 27. = _____ | 24. = _____ | 31. = _____ | 26. = _____ |
| 30. = _____ | 28. = _____ | 32. = _____ | 29. = _____ |
| Total: _____ | Total: _____ | Total _____ | Total _____ |

*Do you find the results interesting, or do you still feel confused?* This assessment is only a guide, not a definitive test. Share your results with your coach, peers, or people who know you best. Ask them if the results seem right to them. You could also take the test again with their help and input, or have them take the test as if they were you. The goal is not to pin you down or define you, but to open you up to various possibilities that resonate with you.

Don't worry about what to do next; I'll help you in the pages ahead. Now that you've completed the assessment, there are two important principles to remember:

1. Your primary influencer voice creates flow.
2. Your influencer voice order creates leverage.

By leaning into these two principles, you'll be able to go further faster. You'll avoid the shiny object syndrome we discussed earlier, and you'll know your best path forward. Let's take a closer look at how you can capitalize on these two principles.

## Your Primary Influencer Voice Creates Flow

Your fastest path to impact and income can be found by leaning into your primary influencer voice. There is no wrong way to build a business, but there is a way that is more right for you.

Embrace how you are naturally wired first. If you are a writer, write. If you are a speaker, speak. If you are a teacher, teach. If you are a coach, then coach. Flow begins to happen when we lean into who we are and how we're naturally wired. To be clear, the assessment you just took is not about competence or skill but more about your core motivations. It reveals to you the way you most prefer to influence others. Flow happens when our goals and motivations come into alignment. Once you begin to master your primary influencer voice, you can begin to leverage the other influencer voices.

## Your Influencer Voice Order Creates Leverage

Just because "writer" may be lowest on your assessment doesn't mean you'll never have a bestselling book. In the pages ahead, I will help you learn how you can be effective in all four areas—speaker, writer, teacher, and coach. The good news is that you can build skills that capitalize on all four influencer voices.

As mentioned earlier, teacher is my primary influencer voice. But over time, I've been able to leverage all four voices—teacher, writer, speaker, and coach—to get my message out to the world.

Still, it makes sense to start with your top influencer voice, as that's the easiest way to start quickly and build momentum. So start by using your primary influencer voice the most. But remember you have other tools in your tool kit, and practice branching out and using the other kinds of influencer voices over time.

As you think about how you want to build your message-based business, go back and look at your assessment results. Rank your influencer voices from highest to lowest. Start with your primary influencer voice and then gain leverage by capitalizing on the other three.

Need a practical example? As mentioned earlier, my influencer voice order is teacher, writer, speaker, and coach. A great path forward for me would be to:

1. Create an online course or membership site (teacher).
2. Use the outline of the course to write and publish a book (writer).
3. Use the content of the book to put together a keynote talk (speaker).
4. Leverage all of the above to create a coaching program (coach).

When we focus first on what comes a bit more naturally, the rest of the process becomes that much easier. The good news is that there are multiple ways to earn income from any of the four influencer voices. One voice is not necessarily better than the others when it comes to the goal of monetizing our message.

Let's take a look at a chart I've created that shows twelve different income streams that stem from our four influencer voices (see figure 7.1).

## The Messenger Product Map

Now that you've identified your primary influencer voice, your fastest path to income and impact can become more clear. The

Messenger Product Map will help you identify how you can use your influencer voice to turn your message into a thriving business. Over the course of my career, I've identified at least twelve income streams that work for any messenger across any industry. In the pages ahead, we'll take a deeper dive into the subject of how you can deploy each income stream into your business. But first, see the following figure for a bird's-eye overview.

7.1

## The Messenger Product Map

| Writer | Speaker |
|---|---|
| Kindle Books<br>Physical Books<br>Audiobooks | Keynote Talks<br>Live Events<br>Workshops |
| **Teacher** | **Coach** |
| Online Courses<br>Membership Site<br>Paid Webinar Series | 1-on-1 Coaching<br>4–6 Week Group Coaching<br>1-Year Paid Mastermind |

## Writer-Based Income Streams

Want to get paid to write? The good news is that you don't have to wait for someone's approval to earn money as an author. In chapter 14 I'll share with you three income opportunities that can be achieved through writing that are available to everyone. You don't even need a website, an audience, or an email list to get started. Just write today and get paid tomorrow. A recent study found that Amazon paid out over $220 million to self-published authors in a single fiscal year. There's an incredible opportunity today for writers to earn money each and every month from their own self-published books.[4]

## Teacher-Based Income Streams

As I've mentioned, I'm a former high school teacher. Both of my parents were educators. I've always admired the teaching profession. Who wouldn't enjoy being able to inspire students to go after their dreams on a daily basis? The challenge was that the traditional teaching model was the wrong context for me. The rigorous schedule, bell-to-bell teaching, and not much discretionary time wore me down.

Maybe you are like me. You have a desire to teach but also have a high need for freedom. If so, I have good news for you. You can get paid to teach on your own terms. I'm not referring to being a teacher for an online educational institution. I'm talking about creating and selling your own courses.

According to *Forbes*, the e-learning industry is expected to climb to over $325 billion over the next decade.[5] While there are many ways to get paid to teach online, my three favorite are online courses, membership sites, and a paid webinar series. As mentioned, we will go into more depth on each of these in a later chapter. For now, just know that if you have the heart of a teacher, there's a real opportunity waiting for you.

## Speaker-Based Income Streams

It's often stated that the fear of public speaking is surpassed only by the fear of death. Still, many people dream of being paid to speak. But that's a job just for well-known celebrities, past presidents, and bestselling authors, right?

No. According to Pete Vargas III of Advance Your Reach, which helps aspiring speakers book speaking gigs, meeting planners are looking to hire speakers across nine major sectors today, including arts and entertainment, business, education, personal finance and wealth, family, government, health and wellness, media, and religion. If you have a passion, there's a stage for you. Public speaking is still a growing profession.[6]

## Coach-Based Income Streams

There is no question the coaching industry is here to stay. People need advice and accountability in all kinds of areas in their lives, and personal and professional coaches are meeting this need with increasing frequency. A person can find coaches in every industry or hobby imaginable. Maybe the coach they need to find is you.

Whether you prefer to work one-on-one or with a group, you can get paid to coach. While coaching can be done in person, it's even more scalable with the internet. Your potential client base is not tied to a geographical region. From the comfort of your own home, you can lead a video-based group-coaching experience that serves attendees from all over the world. According to the Market Research Blog, the personal coaching industry recently topped $1 billion in revenue in the United States alone.[7] There's no sign of this trend slowing down anytime soon. It doesn't matter the topic or industry. People will gladly pay you for what you know.

## Combine Your Unique Gift with Your Influencer Voice

Before we move on, let's apply what we've covered so far to get a picture of your best you in action. You do this by combining your unique gift with your influencer voice. Let's look at my life as an example. My key word is *resourceful*, and my primary influencer voice is *teacher*. Therefore, I can narrow the essence of how I best show up to *resourceful teacher*. By combining my unique gift (resourcefulness) and my primary influencer voice (teaching), I have a powerful combination to launch and grow my message-based business. Other people may come up with combinations such as

- positive writer
- charismatic speaker
- insightful coach
- innovative teacher

The point is to have fun with this exercise. The possibilities are endless. Find two words that excite, motivate, and empower you. If you don't have those two words nailed down, go back to the beginning of this chapter and go through the exercises again. Also, this word combination should touch you at a deeper level. When you find it you may experience emotions you haven't felt in a long time. It could even bring tears to your eyes as you realize (possibly for the first time) you do have value to offer the world. If you don't express your gift, what will the world miss out on? How might the world look different if you live out this best version of yourself? And how will you feel different if you do?

One way to cement this way of thinking in your mind is through what author and professor Timothy Wilson calls the "George Bailey Technique."[8] The one movie I watch with my family every Christmas season is *It's a Wonderful Life*. In this film, after a series of unfortunate events, the character George Bailey comes to the false conclusion that the world would be better off without him. In an effort to stop George from ending his life, Clarence the angel comes down from heaven to teach him an important lesson. Clarence's approach is unique. Instead of trying to cheer George up by having him count his blessings, he shows him an alternate storyline. What would the world be like if George Bailey never existed? For the first time, George sees what the world looks like when his influence is taken away. His wife never married, which means his kids were never born. The small town he lived in, Bedford Falls, changed for the worse. It was overrun with bars and casinos. It lost its small-town feel. The world is far worse off without the influence of George Bailey.

And so it is with you, my friend. What will the future world be like if you don't spread your influence? We need you to express your gift! Your gift is needed in the world.

Now that you have uncovered your purpose by identifying your unique gift and influencer voice, it's time to find your people. Who do you want to serve? Who is your ideal audience? What group of people are you excited to get deeply acquainted with? Finding our people is one of the most exciting steps in this whole process. Let's get started!

# The Messenger Roadmap

## *Your Message Defined (Purpose)*

It's time to add to your Messenger Roadmap again. In this exercise, we'll take three steps. If you completed the earlier two exercises, you should already have the answers to the first two steps below.

Step 1. *What is your unique gift?* My unique gift is
_____.

Step 2. *What is your primary influencer voice?* My primary influencer voice is _____.

Step 3. *Define your message.* The goal over the next few chapters is to help you define your message in a single sentence. The following sentence will help you to define your purpose, people, and passion:

I help _____ (people) to _____ (passion) by being a _____ (purpose).

Combine your unique gift and your primary influencer voice together now and place it in the "purpose" blank above. For example, mine is "resourceful teacher." We will fill out the other blanks in the chapters ahead. You're doing great work. Let's keep it going!

# 8

# People

## *Who Do You Want to Help?*

Crystal was first introduced to the practice of couponing by her mother. As a homeschool student, Crystal was given a unique and practical assignment. She was placed in charge of the cooking, grocery shopping, and menu-planning for their family of nine while she was still a teenager. She learned the skill of saving money while she was still living at home and afterward carried it on into her marriage. In an effort to stay out of debt while her husband went to law school, Crystal leveraged her knowledge of couponing. In the early 2000s she was able to get her budget for groceries and household products down to just $35 per week.

In 2006, she published an article on her blog sharing advice and knowledge of couponing with others. Much to her surprise, she was quickly inundated with questions from readers from around the world. That's when Crystal Paine found her tribe. The people she most wanted to serve were other money-saving moms. That's the story of how MoneySavingMom.com was born. Within its first year, it became the most visited website in the personal finance genre.[1] Crystal had found the people whose lives she could improve. It's time to ask who is out there waiting for you.

I know you want to help everybody. Most people who start message-based businesses do. But it's important to recognize that when we try to help everyone, we're heard by no one. To be successful with a message-based business, you must do two things: choose a specific audience to serve and find a specific problem to solve. In this chapter, we'll focus on your audience.

## Choose a Specific Audience to Serve

Instead of trying to be a career and life coach for everyone when I first started in the business, I chose to work with accounting and finance professionals. By narrowing my focus to a specific audience, I was able to make my communication more targeted, and thus more powerful. Whenever an accounting or finance professional visited my site, they instantly thought, *This is for me!* If no one is raising their hand and exclaiming "This is for me!" when they come across your message, then you haven't yet defined your audience.

To get even more specific in my search for accounting and finance clients, I also decided to pursue a particular egoic label. Egoic labels are the labels people use to identify or describe themselves. Some common egoic labels we all recognize include golfer, hunter, entrepreneur, dog owner, cat lover, single mom, grandmother, and Mac user. Egoic labels tend to be very specific instead of general.

For example, the egoic label I chose to target for my first blog was CPA (Certified Professional Accountant). I positioned myself as the CPA Career Coach. Accountants who have earned the CPA designation are proud of it and often refer to themselves as a CPA. You know you've found a strong egoic label when people use the term to describe themselves. Have you ever heard the term AFOL?

It's an acronym that stands for "adult fan of LEGO." The term has become an egoic label. Adults who still enjoy building with LEGOs love the term. Let's walk through a simple way to use egoic labels to narrow down your ideal audience.

## The Audience Filter Scorecard

Have too many ideas? Still not sure which of your ideas you should build a business around? I have another exercise for you. I call it the Audience Filter Scorecard. When it comes to choosing an audience, we often only look at it from an emotional standpoint. We get stuck on thinking about who we think we should want to serve instead of who we're best suited to serve. This exercise will help to infuse some logic and analytical thinking into the process of finding which audience you should pursue.

Start by completing this sentence with the first three ideas or egoic labels that come to mind:

"I want to help _____ , _____ , and _____ ."

Examples might include elementary school teachers, single moms, baseball card collectors, fathers of teenage boys, accounting professionals, Christian singles, or women entrepreneurs just to name a few. Once you've written down your first three ideas, I want you to run each of them through the following six filtering questions. Let's work through the questions first, then I'll give you a chart to fill in to complete the exercise.

### 1. Do I enjoy learning about this egoic label?

As crazy as it sounds, many entrepreneurs never stop to ask themselves this question. All they want to know is which opportunity will make them the most money. But in order to build a successful message-based business, you must be a *leading learner*. A leading learner is someone who never stops learning about a topic or group of people. Leading learners have a never-ending curiosity about a subject. Always having something new to say on a topic is the thing that will keep you interesting to your ideal audience. You'll also become resourceful in the process. You'll be well equipped to provide answers or insights at a moment's notice.

If you have zero desire to become a leading learner on a topic linked to a particular egoic label, you may want to tap on the brakes. Which topic *do* you have a never-ending curiosity about? What egoic label is associated with that topic? Go ahead and scratch out the rejected egoic label and try this new one instead.

### 2. Am I passionate about this egoic label?

Passion should never be the sole reason you pursue a niche, but it does play an important role in building a business. Passion gives you a deep emotional well to draw from in the early stages of your business. When you lack feedback, income, results, and testimonies, passion keeps you going. All messengers must travel through the valley of obscurity. You don't wait until you reach the mountaintop of running a successful message-based business to add value and help others. You reach the mountaintop by creating value for others when no one is watching. What keeps us writing, creating, and sharing in the early stages of our business is our passion.

### 3. Do I have experience or skills related to this egoic label?

You don't have to wait to be an expert to launch your business, but you do need to have some experience. I once met a budding entrepreneur at a business conference meet and greet. While chatting we asked one another what types of business we run. He shared with me his passion for helping others learn to do organic gardening in their own backyard. When I asked him about his experience with organic gardening, his answer surprised me. "Oh, I've never gardened before in my life. I thought people would be more interested in following a complete newbie." He was serious.

Now, I'm not saying he cannot be successful. There are exceptions to every rule. In fact, I think he may find success in interviewing the top-ten organic gardeners and distilling their best practices into a few short steps to share with his readers. But as a general rule, you want to lean into topics with which you have some experience or skill.

In Brendon Burchard's book *The Millionaire Messenger*, he shares that there are three kinds of experts:

- The Results Expert—You teach and serve others through the lessons and results you've achieved in life.
- The Research Expert—You have interviewed experts and have done more research than others have on a particular topic.
- The Role Model—You've built up so much trust, respect, and admiration that people pay you for all kinds of advice.[2]

You'll need to fall into one of these three categories if you are going to be a success.

### 4. Does this egoic label have a problem to solve?

Entrepreneurs get paid to solve problems. Your products and services are the solution. That's the first part of the equation. But that's not all that's needed. You may be passionate and knowledgeable on a topic, but if there's no problem to solve, it will be difficult for you to build a profitable business.

One of the first questions you should ask before building a message-based business is this: Are the people you want to serve searching for answers online? Are they consuming blogs, podcasts, and videos? Are they actively consuming content? Are they searching for answers to their burning questions by way of search engines? With a little bit of online research, you can quickly determine if there is demand for experts in your niche.

### 5. Are other businesses earning money helping this egoic label?

Most budding entrepreneurs think success must be found by identifying a market in which there is zero competition. I can't tell you how many times I've been told, "Jonathan, I've done my research and no one is talking about this. I think it presents a huge opportunity for me." But where they see opportunity, I see caution.

Entrepreneur and investor Kevin O'Leary of *Shark Tank* fame says, "Pioneers get shot; settlers get rich." In other words, you don't want to be the first in a new market. You want to plant your business in a growing, yet established marketplace. Heading into uncharted waters may be okay for a company with millions of dollars of venture capital, but it's generally not a good idea for the rest of us.

If you can find evidence that others are making money in your area of interest, that's proof that a market exists. You want to see that people are enrolling in online courses, membership sites, and coaching programs in your niche. That they are buying books and attending events on your topic. The evidence that others are earning money in this field is proof that you can do it too.

### 6. Do I want to serve this egoic label?

You must fall in love with the people you want to serve. This doesn't mean that you will like everyone you work with. But in order to truly serve people, you must love them first. Does your heart go out to them? Do you feel pain on their behalf? Do you empathize with the struggles they are going through? Are you willing to walk a mile in their shoes to better understand their goals, passions, and struggles? To truly serve an audience you must be willing to become deeply acquainted with them.

## Choosing Your Audience

Now that we've covered the questions in detail, it's time to do the exercise. Take your top three ideas or egoic labels through the Audience Filter Scorecard below. Taking one idea at a time, walk through the six filtering questions. Your answer should be a rating between 1 and 10 (10 being the highest). Then tally your final score.

## The Audience Filter Scorecard

| I want to help . . . | Egoic Label 1 | Egoic Label 2 | Egoic Label 3 |
|---|---|---|---|
| 1. Do I enjoy *learning* about this egoic label? | /10 | /10 | /10 |
| 2. Am I *passionate* about this egoic label? | /10 | /10 | /10 |
| 3. Do I have *experience* or skills related to this egoic label? | /10 | /10 | /10 |
| 4. Does this egoic label have a *problem to solve*? | /10 | /10 | /10 |
| 5. Are other *businesses earning money* helping this egoic label? | /10 | /10 | /10 |
| 6. Do I want to *serve* this egoic label? | /10 | /10 | /10 |
| **Total Score:** | /60 | /60 | /60 |

Once you've filled out each section completely, tally your scores in the final row. The highest possible score is a sixty. How do the three egoic labels, or potential target audiences, compare? When analyzing your results, keep the following things in mind:

1. The higher the score, the greater the opportunity for you.
2. Go with your gut in the event of any tied scores.
3. If you're still stumped, consider asking a peer or coach for their input.

## Analyzing Your Results

Which of your ideas came out on top? Were you able to identify a clear winner? There is no right or wrong answer. The goal of this simple exercise is to help you think *logically* about the audience you should choose to serve first. When pursuing our passions, it's easy to let our emotions rule. Emotions do play a part, but they're not the whole of our concerns. We also should look at our different passions in a logical way. Doing so will keep you grounded.

Now that you've uncovered your unique gift (your purpose) and discovered the people you most want to serve, including those you'll target with your message first (your people), it's time to identify which problem you want to solve (your passion).

# The Messenger Roadmap

## *Your Message Defined* (*People*)

Congratulations, your message is coming together! You're ready to fill in another section of the Messenger Roadmap. Let's take the following two steps:

Step 1. *Who do you want to help?* The egoic label I want to help is _____.

Step 2. *Define your message further.* In the last chapter you defined your purpose. Go ahead and fill it in again here. And now it's time to add your people to the statement below.

I help _____ (people) to _____ (passion) by being a _____ (purpose).

Awesome! There's only one more part to go to fully define your message. Let's discover your passion!

# 9

# Passion

## What Problem Will You Solve?

At nineteen years of age, Kimanzi Constable started his own business as a bread truck deliveryman in Milwaukee, Wisconsin. As he began to learn the business, his opportunities for advancement grew, but so did the workload. It wasn't unusual for Kimanzi to put in an eighty-hour workweek. While he was considered successful in the eyes of most in his industry, the work he was doing just wasn't his passion. The long hours wore on him, and at times he wondered why he was working so hard.

Then one day, during one of his daily routes, he discovered podcasts. He found listening to them to be an enjoyable way to learn while working his delivery route. While listening to podcasts, he began to hear the stories of people who were building online businesses. They were earning good money and making a difference in the lives of others while enjoying more freedom of time. Freedom was the missing element for Kimanzi. He wanted more than anything to run a business that would give him his freedom back.

## From Bread Truck Deliveryman to International Consultant

In 2011 he took a leap. He started by writing and self-publishing his first book. It only sold five copies in the first six months. Kimanzi was discouraged to say the least, but he didn't let that stop him. He hired coaches, enrolled in courses, and immersed himself in the process of learning how to sell books and build an audience online. By the end of 2012, his lifestyle business was beginning to generate $5,000 a month.

While he still had much to learn, Kimanzi kept putting in the time and effort to build his business. Since podcasting had been so instrumental to his professional growth, he decided to make building his business through podcast interviews his new strategy. Over the next several months, he was interviewed on over eighty podcasts as a guest and his brand began to grow. He also saw an opportunity to be a guest contributor on blogs, so he wrote and published over sixty guest blog posts.

Today, Kimanzi is the author of four books that have sold more than 150,000 copies. He's a regular contributor to major media outlets such as the *Huffington Post*, *Entrepreneur*, *Success* magazine, and *Business Insider*. Over the last five years, he has booked hundreds of thousands of dollars in international consulting contracts and traveled to over seventy-eight countries.[1] Kimanzi traded in his delivery truck to follow his passion.

## How to Find Your Passion in Life

When it comes to college planning, most college-bound kids get funneled in one of two directions. First is the safe and secure job route. They are told that the wise thing to do is to find a career in a field that offers security and good pay. Get a college degree in a certain field and only choose work that lines up with your college degree. To do any different would be to commit career suicide.

The problem with this line of thinking is that those careers—ones with guaranteed security and good pay—no longer exist. The world is changing at a much faster rate than decades ago. Companies come and go. They downsize, restructure, and outsource. The only thing you can count on anymore is change.

The second approach is to find their one and only calling. Students are told to find a path they can dedicate the rest of their lives to. The question is usually phrased this way: "What do you want to do with your life?" Talk about a loaded question!

Asking a college-bound young person this question often results in added pressure and constant procrastination. Some feel pigeonholed into certain degrees by other people. Still others stay undecided because they are unsure of what type of career they'd enjoy. Who's to know what new careers will be invented in the next few decades? A few years ago social media didn't even exist. Today, companies pay good money to hire social media managers.

I know I couldn't have gone to college for what I'm doing today. It wasn't even invented yet. So how do you discover your purpose in a world that is constantly changing? You do so by discovering what is changeless about *you*.

Remember, you don't find your purpose in life, you uncover it. It's an inward journey, not an external pursuit. Many people confuse purpose and passion. The two things are altogether different. The truth is that you'll have many different passions over your lifetime. But your purpose will never change.

## Passions Change, but Your Purpose Endures

*Passion* is an often misunderstood word. People mistakenly believe they must find their one and only passion in life. But finding your passion should not feel like pressure. If you find yourself frustrated or even paralyzed when it comes to choosing your calling, then write these six words down now: *Passions change, but your purpose endures.* You very well may have six to eight different passions over your lifetime, and that's okay. You are not a wandering child. You are not someone who lacks focus. You are not doomed to failure as a person who can't seem to stick with any one thing. Having lots of passions is normal; that's how it should be.

At the same time, as we learned in a previous chapter, you've been given a unique gift. Living out that gift is living out your purpose in life. Unlike passions, which you can have lots of, you have only one purpose. I can throw you into any career context and you will navigate toward your purpose (otherwise known as your unique gift). It doesn't matter what your job description says. You can't help it. It's how you are wired.

Most people will pursue many different passions over their lifetime, but their unique gift, or how they best show up to solve a specific problem, will always look much the same. A much better question to ask yourself than *What do I want to do with my life?* is *Which problem am I most passionate about solving right now?* Doesn't that question feel better? There's less pressure attached to it. Which problem are you most passionate about solving right now? Which problem are you willing to dedicate the next two to five years to solving? These questions will bring you much closer to identifying the passion you should pursue now.

When it comes to nailing down your passion, there are two key steps you'll need to take:

1. Identify a core human need you want to address.
2. Choose a specific problem to solve.

## Which of These Six Core Human Needs Does Your Business Address?

Did you know you can solve problems for money? People pay other people to solve their problems. Your audience has needs, wants, and desires, and you can help them with all three.

After working with thousands of message-based entrepreneurs over the years, I've come to the conclusion that there are six core human needs. Almost every message-based business is helping their audience solve problems in one or more of the following areas: identity, health, wealth, relationships, spirituality, and wisdom. In light of the audience you selected in the last chapter, which of these six core human needs do you want to address?

### Identity

We all want to live lives that matter. We want to feel like we have something valuable to contribute in this world. We want to have a voice. We want to matter to other people. We want to be loved and cared for. We want to be told we have a special gift and that it's needed in the world. Helping others stand firm in their identity can be some of the most rewarding work you can pursue. Will your business help others in shaping a powerful identity? Top-of-mind problems in this area include feeling a lack of confidence, having an unbalanced life, or experiencing a lack of purpose.

### Health

We want to live with energy and vitality. We want to have an active lifestyle well into our old age. We want the good report from the doctor. We want to eat right and feel good. Are you able to help others with their need to achieve better health? Obvious signs of a lack of health include lack of energy, a poor health report, being overweight, and chronic headaches. These are just some examples of problems people can have that fall into this category.

## Wealth

Most of us also desire some level of wealth. We may not all describe it the same way, but the category of wealth includes stability, security, abundance, prosperity, net worth, and fortune. Does your business help others create wealth in some way? Perhaps you can assist them in earning money in a way that allows them more freedom to spend time with their family. Or you can help others build more wealth in order to contribute in areas that are under-resourced. Maybe you have an expertise in a specific type of investing or a wealth creation strategy you want to teach others. Typical problems people may experience in the wealth category include too much personal debt, a lack of retirement planning, the need for career advancement help, and chaotic personal finances.

## Relationships

Do we really need other people in order to live and survive in this life? That was the big question the reality show *Castaways* wanted to address. The ABC television show rounded up twelve willing participants from across the United States to participate in a social experiment. Each contestant was separately scattered on a remote island in Indonesia. The contestants did not know when they were going to be rescued, nor did they know where the other contestants were located.

The social experiment was simple: in the midst of challenging circumstances, would a person tough it out on their own or would they seek out human companionships? As each episode aired, the answer became clear: people need human relationships. Looking back on his experience on the show, contestant Richard Rogers came to this conclusion: "You need people to survive [the game], and the same with life, you need people in life to survive."[2]

Relationships are another fundamental core human need we all have. Does your business speak to the relational challenges others face with their marriage partner, extended family, or friends? Relationship issues exist as long as there are people around. Typical problem areas in this category include an inability to perform well at work, emotional instability, conflict and drama, and financial issues.

### Spirituality

Many people are searching for deeper answers to life beyond their physical needs. The proof of this is found in the number of different religions around the world. Through your writing, speaking, and coaching, you can lead others into a deeper, more meaningful life. In the category of spirituality, people need practical help with the problems of feeling disconnected, feeling a lack of purpose, and feeling weighed down by guilt and despair.

### Wisdom

If there's one problem I hear brought up the most, it has to be either a lack of time or the inability to make good decisions. In today's fast-paced world we live life with no margin for error. There's more to do than time available in our schedules to do it.

Helping people to uncover where they are wasting time and learn how to be more productive can be extremely rewarding work. Obvious signs of a lack of time include feeling overwhelmed, an inability to push forward on important goals, the practice of overpromising and underdelivering, and lack of making good decisions. Wisdom for living informs how we spend our days and how we make important choices.

Another way to understand the six core human needs is shown in the following graphic. The need for identity is at the very center. I believe at the core of every human life is the question, *Why am I here?* At the second level we find spirituality, wealth, health, and relationships. These represent the different categories of needs we have in our daily lives. Finally, we see wisdom represented as the outer circle. How we spend our days and the choices we make affect all the other areas of our lives.

9.1

**The Six Core Human Needs**

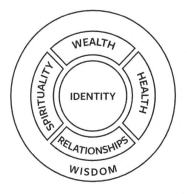

It's important to note that your business does not need to address all six human needs to be successful. Truthfully, you can find success by addressing just one of the core needs. It's also okay if your business addresses more than one core need. The point of this exercise is to identify that your business intends to meet at least one of these six core needs. Regardless of what niche, demographic, or worldview you have, always speak to at least one of these six needs.

## Choose a Specific Problem to Solve

I'd easily win the award for the strangest Little League photo as a kid. When I was in first grade, I came down with chicken pox. Yes, the kind that is super contagious. Yet even though I was contagious, for some strange reason my parents still drove me to participate in my Little League team photo. I have that picture to this day. Holding a bat, in uniform, with full-on chicken pox. One could argue that maybe I was past the point of being contagious. I hope so.

Still, my problem was obvious to everyone who saw me. There I was out on the field in full uniform, as if I were ready to play. But that day I wasn't in need of a home-run swing. I needed to get rid of the chicken pox. Before I could really play, I needed to solve my obvious problem.

The same is true for building your business. It's natural for us as speakers, writers, and coaches to dive into issues related to systems, techniques, and tools without first addressing the most obvious problem. As I mentioned earlier, my first blog was written for accounting and finance professionals. The specific problem I chose to solve was job transition. I wanted to help accountants who felt stuck in their current role find a new, more meaningful job with a new company. Because I'd defined a specific problem to solve, I didn't have to be all things to all people. I didn't talk much about how to get a promotion, how to handle a difficult boss, or how to get the CPA certification. Instead I focused on topics related to making a job change. Because of that, I became known as a specialist who could help accountants find better work.

Once you've identified a core human need to address, it's time to niche down to a specific problem. What's the best way to choose a specific problem to solve? Think of a top-of-mind symptom your audience is experiencing.

People often don't know the cause of their problems, but they know their symptoms. When you are not feeling well and go to the doctor, the doctor always starts by asking about your symptoms. And you identify them. I have a sore throat. I have constant headaches.

The point is that our communication becomes stronger when we describe the symptoms our audience is facing. For example, therapists identifying the problems they help solve shouldn't say, "I help people feel better by using cognitive behavioral therapy." That's the solution. Instead, they should talk about a specific problem or the symptom. A better way to frame the statement would be, "I help people overcome feelings of depression." Doesn't this statement feel more relatable?

To be an effective communicator, you need to speak to the symptom or the specific problem your audience is facing. Using this example, let's look at one way a therapist might niche down his or her message.

1. I help people to improve their core identity [core need].
2. I help people to feel better by using cognitive behavioral therapy [solution].
3. I help people to overcome feelings of depression [specific problem].

Do you see how much more powerful the last statement is? Picture the response someone might have after you say, "I help people feel better by using cognitive behavioral therapy." Their response might be, "Oh, that's nice." But when you tell that same person, "I help people overcome feelings of depression in thirty days or less," it feels different doesn't it? Describing the symptom is more relatable, and it's attached to a specific problem your audience is facing.

## Combining Purpose, People, and Passion into a Powerful Message

Congratulations! You have now walked through the entire Ignite Your Message Framework. By making decisions in three core areas, you have defined your message. The completion of this legwork will make the rest of the process easier. You should now be able to answer three fundamental questions:

- Purpose: What is your unique gift?
- People: Who do you want to help?
- Passion: What problem will you solve?

Now that you have defined your message, it's time to establish your home base. In the next chapter, I'll share with you some of the best practices for building a dynamic website even if you are technologically challenged.

# The Messenger Roadmap

## Your Message Defined (*Putting It All Together*)

All right, now we get to place the final piece into our puzzle—our passion. If you've done the previous exercises on our roadmap, go ahead and fill in the blanks for purpose and people. Next, complete the sentence by filling in the passion statement you crafted from the exercises in this chapter.

I help _____ (people) to _____ (passion) by _____ (purpose).

Jonathan's example: I help online entrepreneurs (what I call *messengers*) to rise above the noise and get their messages heard by being a resourceful teacher.

# 10

# Mission Control

## *Establishing Your Home Base*

For our twenty-first wedding anniversary, my wife and I spent a week in New York City. On the third day of our visit, we decided to do a bit of exploring in Central Park. The park is conveniently located right in the middle of the "city that never sleeps." Most people are surprised by the park's massive size when they see it for the first time. Its rolling 842 acres offer plenty of room to explore, go for a jog, or just enjoy some peace and quiet. I've had the opportunity to explore Central Park a few times. Every time I go, I experience a new section of the park I've never seen before.

As my wife and I were walking through the middle of the park, we came around a bend and saw something that stopped us in our tracks. It was a 130-foot-high Victorian-style castle known as Belvedere Castle. We noticed people were in the castle, so we decided to take a closer look. We navigated our way through cobbled paths and old stone-carved winding staircases until we finally reached the top. We were standing at Central Park's second-highest elevation point, the first being Summit Rock. The view was breathtaking.

Once we got back to the hotel, I decided to do a bit of research on the castle. I had questions about how the castle got there and why it was even built in the first place. It turns out the name Belvedere means "beautiful view" in Italian. That certainly seemed like the right name for that castle.

As I investigated further, I discovered the reason the castle was built was to be a folly. That seemed strange to me. I associate the word *folly* as meaning useless, a waste, or foolish. As I looked deeper into the story, I realized I wasn't far off in my assessment. A Victorian Folly, as it's known, is a structure whose main function is to be ornamental, serving no practical use and without an intended purpose. And for many years, that's the role this castle served. In fact, in the 1960s, Belvedere Castle was closed to the public and became known as a symbol of neglect, deterioration, and vandalism.[1] Luckily, that's not the end of the story.

Following a $12 million renovation that concluded in 2019, the castle today serves as a visitor center and gift shop. It's estimated that this once desolate castle now hosts over a million tourists each year. Just like Belvedere Castle, your home base, your website, can also have one of two outcomes. It can fail and waste your resources, or it can succeed and serve as a place of service.

## Creating a Website to Launch to the World

There are only two ways to create a website. And frankly, one works, the other doesn't. One kind of website serves like a Victorian Folly and the other as a money-making tourist attraction. Without realizing it, most people build a website the way a person might build a folly. How so, you ask? They focus on advertising their qualifications instead of demonstrating their expertise.

When we only focus on advertising our qualifications, we make the website about us and our credentials. But there's a better way. It starts by understanding there's a big difference between *displaying* your expertise and *demonstrating* your expertise.

### Option 1: Displaying Your Expertise

Most online entrepreneurs begin with the static brochure website strategy. You can find these all over the internet. A static brochure consists of five to ten webpages focused on displaying the certifications and credentials of the expert. The website is heavily focused on the expert as the hero. It's no different than taking a hard-copy brochure and displaying it online. The emphasis is on pages labeled *about me, view my work, work with me, contact us,* or the equivalent. Once the branding and expertise are well displayed on the website, no more content is added to the site.

A person with a static brochure website next faces a perplexing marketing question: "How do I get visitors to my website?" It doesn't take them long to figure out that when they stop marketing their site, people stop showing up. Over time they become frustrated with marketing in general. Without even realizing it, they've turned marketing into sales.

Selling yourself day in and day out is exhausting. The only way out of this downward spiral is to stop trying to be the hero. As we already discussed in chapter 5, the real hero is your audience. You are just the guide. It's time to start acting like one.

### Option 2: Demonstrating Your Expertise

What do Yoda, Mr. Miyagi, and Gandalf all have in common? They deflect the attention away from themselves and focus on the mission at hand. Their aim in life is not to display their credentials or even make the story about them. Their goal is solely found in guiding others and making them the hero. They accomplish their mission by demonstrating their expertise using the forms of lessons, questions, challenges, goals, and advice. Luke Skywalker didn't ask Yoda if his Jedi certification was up to date. Nor did Daniel, the Karate Kid, inquire about the qualification of Mr. Miyagi's karate experience. Your audience wants your help, not your diploma.

And here's the best part: demonstrating your knowledge has never been easier. One of the best ways to become a guide for your audience is to fully embrace content marketing. *Content marketing* is a term that refers to the free content we'll discuss in detail in the next section of the book. But for now, simply know this: a major benefit of free content is that you can add value to people's lives whether they buy from you or not. Content marketing also embraces the idea that this free content can lead to sales. It refers to the process by which you gain customers or clients via your blog posts, podcasts, or videos.

When you use content marketing, your website is not static but dynamic. Every single week you add new, valuable content that offers insight, guidance, and help. Over time, you develop a beautiful body of work that guides others down the path they need to go. Articles, podcasts, and even videos you recorded years ago are discovered by new prospects who are just finding out about you. As you build trust via the "give value first" strategy, sales in your business become the natural by-product.

## Five Must-Haves for Every Messenger's Website

Now that you understand the two major differences between the two kinds of websites, let's get more practical about what a messenger's website should offer. How do we create a website that instantly connects with our ideal reader? How do we keep visitors on our site for long periods of time? How do we communicate our message in such a way that it draws people to join our email list? While your website can serve many different functions, I believe there are five primary features every messenger's website should include.

### 1. A Concise, Aspirational Headline

The first thing a visitor should notice when they visit your home page is a headline that instantly connects. The best type of headline is one that is less than ten words and aspirational in nature. What's aspirational? A statement that inspires them toward a goal, desire, or status they want to achieve.

When I did a ten-minute brainstorm, I came up with the following aspirational headlines:

- Transform Your Passion into a Platform.
- Discover Your Message. Launch Your Platform.
- Discover Your Hidden Genius. Do Work that Matters.
- Work from Anywhere. Influence People Everywhere.
- Uncover Your Unique Gift. Make an Impact on the World.

Do any of those headlines connect with you? My guess is yes or you wouldn't be reading this book. It's good to come up with more than one headline because you can always use some of the other headlines on other pages on your site. For example, you might display one on your "about me" page and another on the "contact us" page. The goal here is to have on your landing page a short aspirational headline that connects with your ideal audience.

### 2. The Big Three Challenges Your Audience Faces

As a guide, you want to show empathy with your audience. You want them to know you understand the challenges and frustrations they face. More than anything, your audience wants to feel heard. One of the best ways to connect with them is by putting into words the challenges they face. I encourage you to come up with three big challenges you can name. Sure, you can come up with more, but at least start with three. A great way to feature these challenges on your website is in the form of questions. Here are a few of mine as examples:

- Overwhelmed by technology challenges?
- Trying to figure out how to rise above the noise?
- Worried about what the critics will say?
- Is the fear of not being good enough stopping you?
- Does your lack of focus feel paralyzing?

What I just listed above are some of the top challenges I hear from my audience on a regular basis. If you are unsure what your audience's challenges might be, just start asking. The more you ask, the more their big three challenges will rise to the surface.

### 3. The Big Three Success Steps You Offer

Another role of being the guide is to have a plan. While it's great to show empathy with your audience by identifying with their challenges, that's only half of the equation. The other half is to show them you have a simple plan that can lead them toward success.

The mistake that many guides make is to have a plan with too many steps. You'll lose your audience by trying to share your twenty-one-point success path. That doesn't mean you have to dumb down your plan and make it overly simplistic. What it means is that, as the guide, you only reveal what needs to be revealed right now.

For example, how can you take your theoretical twenty-one-point success path and divide it into three phases? It's much easier to understand and remember three phases than it is to digest a twenty-one-point plan. We as guides can share more details later as the customer goes deeper into the program. Here's an example of a plan I would offer on my website:

- Step 1. Discover Your Message
- Step 2. Launch Your Platform
- Step 3. Grow Your Tribe

Do you see how it's easier to communicate just three steps to reach success? If you had to break down a success plan for your audience into just three steps, what would they be? Write those three steps down and display them on the home page of your website.

### 4. A Direct Call to Action to Subscribe

As you'll learn in the pages ahead, I'm a big believer in building an email list. An email list of followers is one of the single most important assets of any business. That's why one of the five most essential ingredients you need to have on your website is a direct call to action.

Also known as CTA, a call to action is an obvious button on your site that displays words such as *Start Here*, *Register Today*, *Download Now*, *Get a Quote*, or *Start a Free Trial*. Your call to action statement should be four words or less and include an action verb if at all possible. I recommend displaying this button on at least one of the following three places on your website:

- *Front and center on your home page*—Your most important real estate on your home page is a section called "above the fold." If you've never heard the term before, it comes from the newspaper industry. In order to sell the most newspapers, an editor made sure to place the best headline of the day on the top half of the first page. That's because it was the most visible section of a newspaper even when the paper was displayed in a newspaper rack. On a website, it's the part of the home page you see before you scroll down.

• *Top menu navigation header*—The navigation header is what you see at the very top of a webpage. It displays links to the most important parts of the website. A great strategy to collect more emails is to have a button that stands out from all the rest of the header menu that has a call-to-action statement.

• *Top right sidebar*—Heat map studies have shown that the most valuable part of a website is typically the top right sidebar. A heat map monitors how visitors interact with a webpage and which part of the webpage they pay attention to most. Think of a sidebar as a column on the right side of a webpage. You typically see these on blogs. The information on the sidebar is the same no matter the webpage. One benefit of placing your call to action button in the right sidebar is that it can be seen no matter what blog post the reader is viewing at the time.

### 5. A Reservoir of Ever-Growing Content

Remember the story of Belvedere Castle? This is where you decide if your website will serve as a "folly" or a successful "tourist attraction." A simple way to create a reservoir of ever-growing content is by regularly publishing posts on your blog. With a blog, you are adding fresh, relevant content on a consistent basis. A blog is not just for writers. A blog post can contain written articles, audio podcasts, and even videos. Simply put, a blog gives your reader a reason to come back. We'll talk more about this in chapter 12, but for now, make a decision to add a blog to your website.

## It's Time to Market Your Message

Why are reality shows so popular? Why are there so many You-Tubers with millions of followers? Because people crave what's real. People want real relationships, real communication, and real emotions. Why? Because people see themselves in these shows. Reality is attractive.

Don't strive to be different; strive to be relevant. Hollywood pushes the idea of being unique and being different. The idea is that the more extreme you are, the more you'll stand out. As a result, many celebrities are living lives of quiet desperation. All the money and fame left them empty inside. Weary from wearing their heavy masks, they silently wonder if their ordinary selves are good enough.

Do you hate selling? You're not alone. The thing that stops a majority of people from sharing their message is their disdain for sales. What if instead of worrying about sales you just focused on being relevant? Being relevant is underrated. People crave what's real. Being yourself is your superpower.

Isn't that refreshing? You don't have to become something you are not. If you are an introvert, you don't have to become an extrovert to have influence on others. Being you is good enough. The way you talk is good enough. The way you think is good enough. The way you look is good enough. You are enough. What you have to offer is enough.

Ditch the doubts.

Stop playing small.

You are just as worthy as anyone else.

Stop selling your product, and start sharing your message. Stop promoting yourself and start promoting your content. Sharing your message will build a tribe. Selling a product will build a reputation. No one likes being sold to, but everyone likes being heard.

When you focus on creating content that targets your audience's goals, passions, and struggles, they feel heard.

You can do that. You just need to help your audience find you so you can be there for them. It's time to learn how to market your message without it sounding like a sales pitch.

# PART 3

# MARKET
# YOUR
# MESSAGE

Have you ever heard of bamboo fishing poles? Picture the kind of fishing pole you imagine Tom Sawyer may have used while fishing in the Mississippi River. A modern-day bamboo fishing pole is a ten-foot-long bamboo stick with fishing line tied to the end. What's unique about it, besides being longer than a standard fishing pole, is that it has no reel. When I was ten years old, my brothers and I were given a set of bamboo fishing poles.

Excited about setting out on a new adventure, we immediately decided to go fishing. Armed with our new poles, we only needed two more things: a place to fish and bait to attract the fish. Since we lived on a forty-acre campground, we had several ponds on the property. But what would we do to solve the bait problem? The only solution we could come up with at the time was to start digging for worms. We found a place in the campground we thought would have worms and began digging. Sure enough, we found plenty. Not having a container to put our bait in and having the reasoning ability of young boys, we decided to use our pants pockets. Later we realized this was a mistake when our mother found the extra worms while checking our pockets before tossing them in the washer. You've never heard such a squeal.

Once we found the bait, we were off to find the best spot to fish. At first, we had little to no luck. Since there were several ponds, though, we remained optimistic that eventually we'd find a perfect fishing spot. And we did. We found a spot where the bluegill bit the moment we placed our poles in the water. Almost instantly we could see our long bamboo poles bend so much we thought they might break. In the span of fifteen minutes, we caught ten or more bluegill. After we caught one, we would toss it back in the pond. It wasn't until later I began to wonder if we just caught the same fish ten times. But what, you may ask, does fishing have to do with building a business? I'll tell you: a lot.

To attract and build an audience with your message, you must learn to go fishing. If only we knew how to find the perfect fishing hole, everything would become easier, or so we think. Finding where your tribe is hanging out online can feel a lot like fishing. Yet even when we, as online entrepreneurs, find our tribe, we still doubt whether it can grow into a profitable business. As one survey responder expressed, "I know I need to find my pond, my tribe, my people who will resonate with my message. But will that pond be big enough to support my message?"

One of the top things messengers desire is to find an audience to serve—a group of people to lead. We lose hope as we wonder where they are and how we can reach them. I've been there. In the not too distant past, I too struggled with how to build an audience with my message. After careful observation of other successful entrepreneurs, though, I made a fascinating discovery. I realized that all successful messengers focus on four keystone habits. They all do these four things exceptionally well. To help you remember these four focusing habits, I've developed a teaching tool we'll talk about in the next chapter. It's known as the Hourglass Funnel.

# 11

# Extraordinary Focus Leads to Success

Forty-four-year-old Dean Potter was about to attempt the impossible. It was April of 2012, and before him stood forty-four yards of rope that stretched over China's Enshi Grand Canyon. The floor of the canyon was more than a mile beneath him.

To complicate matters, Dean wasn't your typical tightrope walker. Rather, his preferred style was slackline walking. Slackline is considered more challenging than the tightrope because the line is not completely taut and is more susceptible to bouncing. On top of that, a slackline walker makes his crossing without the aid of a safety leash or balancing pole. But Dean Potter successfully made his crossing in just under two minutes. What allowed Dean to make the successful crossing is the same thing we can employ in our business: extraordinary focus.[1]

## The Four Focusing Habits of Successful Messengers

Most creative entrepreneurs are simply overwhelmed. There are too many strategies, tactics, and formulas begging for their attention. As we've already established, as entrepreneurs, we don't suffer from not having enough options. We suffer from having too many.

By nature, I'm a learner. I love to read books, take courses, and attend conferences. Whether these practices come naturally to you or not, these habits can help you too. Investing in yourself and developing your own personal growth is important. But there is also a downside to being a learner. It's easy to get overwhelmed when it comes to implementing what one has learned. It's tempting to try to do it all. But it's impossible to implement everything you learn, and you shouldn't try.

When I analyzed the working habits of the most successful creative entrepreneurs, I observed that they focus on just four things. That's it. They became successful marketing their message because they made a conscious choice to do four things well. Once I started implementing these same four habits, my business grew.

If you are overwhelmed with where to best spend your time to grow your business, let's solve this for you once and for all. Let's look at the four things that you, as a creative entrepreneur, need to be able to do well.

- create
- capture
- compile
- connect

I'll explain in a moment what I mean by these four words. But for now, I want to emphasize why these four words matter: if you practice these four habits consistently, your message will grow.

When I first began to implement these focused habits, I was only able to devote two hours a day to my business. That may not sound like enough, but sure enough, my business began to grow. When I sat down to work in those two hours, I was working on the right things and so I got results.

Growing your business is not about getting everything right, but about doing the right things. Consistency in those right things builds momentum. For your message to grow, you just need to get focused on the things that matter most.

## The Messenger's Hourglass Funnel

To help further explain why these four habits—create, capture, compile, and connect—are so powerful, I've developed a teaching tool I call the Hourglass Funnel. Picture an old-fashioned hourglass that is wide at both the top and the bottom but narrow in the middle and open at the top. The grains of sand represent the people you want to help. People come into your world at the top of the hourglass and work their way to the bottom. All four habits work together to create synergy in your business. If any one of these elements is missing, you will struggle to grow your business.

For example, what's the use of publishing regular blog posts (create habit) if you're not also focused on capturing leads for your business (capture habit)? What's the use of capturing leads for your business (capture habit) if you never have anything to sell them (compile habit)? These are just a few examples, but I could offer many more. Let's take a closer look at each of the four focusing habits in the context of the hourglass illustration.

11.1
### Hourglass Funnel

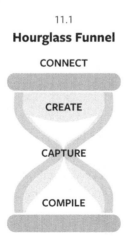

CONNECT

CREATE

CAPTURE

COMPILE

### The Create Habit

The very top of our hourglass is wide and represents how people come into our sphere of influence. The create habit is all about providing free, valuable content in the form of text, audio, and video.

Think about the influencers you follow. You probably didn't begin your journey with them by purchasing an expensive coaching package. More than likely you were hooked by a blog post, podcast, or video that contained value.

Create value first. Value comes before trust. If you skip over this step, you miss an opportunity to build trust and authority with your audience. The type of content you create is based on two factors.

First, you want to lean into your area of strength. As we learned earlier, writers should write; speakers should speak; teachers should teach; and coaches should coach. Your fastest path to impact is directly connected to your primary influencer voice.

Second, you should ask, *What type of content is my ideal audience consuming?* If you don't know the answer to that question, we'll share some ways to find it in the pages ahead. The point is, if your audience doesn't tend to listen to podcasts, don't start a podcast. Find another media outlet that matches your primary influencer voice. What's the purpose of creating all of this free content? The answer is found in the capture habit.

### The Capture Habit

The middle of the hourglass is narrow and represents the skill of capturing leads for your business. There are a variety of ways to do this, which we'll discuss in chapter 13. It doesn't matter which specific tactic you choose, as long as you can do one thing: *build a relationship through ongoing communication using an asset you own.*

While social media is a great tool for reaching your audience, it does not apply here. You don't have 100 percent control of your social media followers. I'm talking about building relationships via an asset that you can control, such as a list of email addresses you own. Your social media accounts could be shut down and your business would still survive because your email list would keep you in business. A list that you own and control is the energy and lifeblood of your business.

Many experts say the money is found in the list. While that's true, there is something more important than money that's also found there. Without that something more, you have no business. The secret ingredient is relationship, and the relationship is in the list.

### The Compile Habit

Once we've built a relationship with our leads, we can now introduce them to our products and services. The bottom of the funnel is where you earn a living. The compile habit is all about packaging your advice and knowledge into products.

You should always be working on something that can generate revenue for you in the days ahead. The good news is that there are many ways to make a living sharing your advice. In fact, I've identified twelve income streams that can be leveraged in any market. We will cover this in-depth in chapter 14. The compile habit will help you to stay focused on the things that generate revenue.

### The Connect Habit

Once you have the top of the funnel (content that creates value), middle of the funnel (ways to capture leads) and bottom of the funnel (ways to sell your knowledge and advice), it's time to pour traffic into your funnel. Picture the top of the funnel with no lid.

The grains of sand represent people, and the connect habit is all about getting new traffic into your funnel.

Once you have created the value-first content, getting traffic becomes easier. Content marketing is all about sharing free value with those who most need it. In the pages ahead, you'll learn the three primary ways to drive traffic—free, paid, and partner sources. Each has it owns advantages and disadvantages, but the eventual goal is to have all three working in your business.

Are you beginning to see how powerful the four focusing habits are in building your business? The reason these four focusing habits bring synergy to your business is that they represent steps in your customer's journey. There's a sequence I developed that all customers of a message-based business follow:

> Value comes before trust, trust comes before attention, attention comes before profits.

## Your Customer's Journey

Once you understand the flow of your customer's journey, everything becomes easier. Capturing leads becomes easier if you've built trust first. Sales become easier once you've built value, trust, and attention. Let's take a close look at how your customer's journey actually works step-by-step.

- *Value comes before trust*. The easiest way to build value is to provide free, helpful content to your audience on a regular basis. As you'll discover in the pages ahead, blogging, podcasting, and vlogging (video blogging) are all content methods you can use to give value with the goal of building trust over time.

- *Trust comes before attention.* One of the main desires of every online entrepreneur is to not only be noticed, but to gain the attention of their audience. The best way to gain attention is to build trust. Trust is built by consistently serving your audience week in and week out. If you've done this well, then gaining attention is easy. For example, if you consistently deliver helpful, insightful emails to your mailing list, they'll open your emails when you send something to them and you'll have their undivided attention.

- *Attention comes before profits.* Once you've gained your audience's undivided attention, profit will more easily flow into your business. All online business owners want more profit, and they want it now. But you can't skip steps in the process and expect to build a sustainable long-term business over time. Yes, there are some strategies that can shorten the journey from value to trust to attention to profits, but the general rule is that you can't skip steps.

An example of a shortcut is webinars. I love to use webinars in my business because they have the power to shorten the customer's journey. Think about it. They gain value by learning from you on a live event. Trust is built because you've delivered the goods. You have their attention because they trust you. And they are more likely to buy from you on the live webinar because they just walked the journey with you. All of the steps happen in a sixty-minute webinar. This formula is what makes the Hourglass Funnel so powerful. It works across all markets and industries.

Over the next few chapters, we'll help you implement the four focusing habits so you can effectively market your message and get paid for what you know. Let's start with the create habit.

# 12

## Create

### Get Your Message Out to the Masses

One of my favorite novels of all time is *A Christmas Carol* by Charles Dickens. Charles Dickens is perhaps one of the most well-known authors of classic literature. But did you know that for years he wrote in obscurity? He spent three years writing for the London-based *Evening Chronicle* for no payment. Then one day, to Dickens's surprise, he was approached by a publisher who wanted to compile his writings into a book. The first print run of *Pickwick Papers* sold five hundred copies, while the last installment sold over forty thousand.[1] Theatrical adaptations were appearing even before he finished writing the series. The same was true for related Pickwick merchandise. Songbooks, china figurines, and Pickwick cigars were sought-after commodities. *The Pickwick Papers* made Charles Dickens the most popular author in the world in 1836.

## We All Start by Creating in Obscurity

Like Charles Dickens, every successful influencer, author, podcaster, or blogger you follow once created their art in complete obscurity. Instead of giving up or being distracted by the latest shiny object, they just kept creating their art. If there is one distinguishing factor between the successful and the unsuccessful content creator, it's that the successful practice their art in public. I first heard of this concept from Jeff Goins in his book *Real Artists Don't Starve*. Jeff shares, "The more we do this [practice in public], the better we get, and the more confident we become. Eventually, people start to notice."[2]

Another way to say it is we launch, then we learn. You don't become a successful writer, then start a blog. Rather you become a great writer while blogging. You don't become a successful podcaster, then start a podcast. You don't wait to become great in front of the camera before starting to record videos. The goal of any endeavor should be to either maximize revenue or maximize learning. Any time you start something new, decide to maximize learning. This can be done only by launching. You launch, and then you learn.

## The Only Three Ways to Create Value Online

The best way to give value first is through creating free content. This is a point we touched on earlier. Most entrepreneurs want to skip over this step to go straight to capturing leads and making sales. Don't make that mistake.

Imagine if building your business was similar to the dating scene. Would you propose marriage on the first date? Of course not. The process of creating and providing content (blogging, podcasting, and videos) allows trust to grow first before any commitment is proposed. Remember, value comes before trust, trust comes before attention, and attention comes before profits. You can't skip a step and build an engaged tribe.

There are only three ways you can give value online. Your audience can either read what you write (blogging), hear what you say (podcasting), or watch what you do (video). Let's look more closely at these three options.

### Your audience reads what you write (blogging).

The written word is as powerful today as it was a hundred years ago. Perhaps even more powerful, in the sense that it shows up in more places and in more forms than ever before. Millions of people daily read the words others have published online. What that means for us is that we don't have to wait for permission to contribute our message.

You can launch a blog and begin to write and share helpful articles today. The only thing stopping you is you. The number one excuse I hear from people who want to start a message-based business is that there is already plenty of good content out there. But don't forget: that other content has been put out there by people who don't have your experience, story, perspective, and personality—your message matters. There are people out there who need exactly the message and help that only you can deliver.

When he was just twenty years old, my friend Bob Lotich decided to go on a seven-month sabbatical. He saw it as a spiritual journey to help him solve some of the deepest questions he was facing. Only one problem. His financial situation was already in dire straits. "I had no savings. I had no money left in my checking account, and my credit card was $264 from being maxed out. My rent was due that day, and I was worried about needing to buy gas to pick up a couple of friends from the airport who would be staying with me that weekend," Bob said.

If that wasn't dire enough, the unthinkable happened. Bob's car broke down. To make matters worse, it broke down right in front of a minor league baseball stadium thirty minutes before game time. Hundreds of cars passed, the drivers staring at his unfortunate predicament. After pushing his car to the side of the road, he climbed back inside, put his head in his hands, and made a commitment to get his finances in order. His financial situation did not change overnight, but his relationship with money did. Bob began to dive deep into books, courses, videos, and articles on personal finance. A little at a time, his financial situation changed for the better.

A few years later he was in a much better place, and he had a burning desire to help others dig their way out of debt and become financially abundant too. But he was unsure how he could take this passion he felt inside and get it out to the world. He decided to create a website where he would post one proverb a day from the book of Proverbs. Since Proverbs has plenty of wisdom on how to make wise choices with money, Bob thought it was a comfortable place to start. While researching how to build his website, he learned that his idea had a name: blogging. A blog was a place he could post regular, helpful articles on personal finance. Every weekday he posted a verse and then posted his ideas about the verse in the form of an article.

As people searched their personal finance questions online, they soon began to find answers from articles Bob had written and posted. Bob found this opportunity to help others to be incredibly energizing. He took all of his life lessons, stories, and financial advice and poured them into daily blog posts. Bob woke up early on Saturday mornings to write five blog posts to schedule out for the coming week. Even though he was still working a corporate job, his blog was growing daily in content and readers.

One day at work, his department was surprised by the news of downsizing. Since Bob had been building his blog business on the side, however, this development was not the crisis it could have been. In fact, he saw an opportunity to take his severance package and go all-in with his blog. Today, *SeedTime* is read by millions of readers every year. Over 200,000 subscribers are on his email list, and it continues to grow. Bob has been featured on major media and news outlets all over the country. All of this was made possible through the power of a blog and the courage to hit Publish.[3]

### Your audience hears what you say (podcasting).

Your followers don't want to just read what you have to say, they also want to hear it. Hearing your voice can bring about a personal, intimate connection that text alone cannot. Your audience can feel the emotion, passion, and compassion behind what you have to say. This is why podcasting is so popular. Your followers can be influenced by you while they're on their morning jog or daily commute.

Jeff Brown spent twenty-six years in traditional radio. He even cohosted an award-winning and nationally syndicated morning show for six years. Even with all of his career success in radio, he always dreamed of one day building his own business. Podcasting became that opportunity. Jeff always had a passion for reading good books. He often wondered what it would be like to have conversations with bestselling authors. He decided to take his passion for radio, start his own podcast, and interview authors on his show.

Since making that decision, Jeff has interviewed several New York Times bestselling authors, including Daniel Pink, Seth Godin, Simon Sinek, John Maxwell, and Liz Wiseman. These connections have led to many more opportunities for Jeff. His *Read to Lead* podcast regularly ranks in the top ten business podcasts in iTunes. His podcast is clearly a success.

But more than just having a popular podcast, Jeff has also built a sustainable business he runs from home. He earns revenue from podcast advertisements and from coaching others on how they too can launch a successful podcast. His podcast has also led to numerous speaking and consulting opportunities, allowing him to teach others what he's learned along his journey about podcasting, leadership, and personal development.[4]

### Your audience watches what you do (video).

Written material and podcasts are great, but many of your followers might learn best visually. Whether it is a screencast of your computer, a PowerPoint slide, or a video of you teaching on the topics you know best, videos can be a powerful medium. Video is powerful because it brings your personality and style closer to your audience. They can better connect with you as a person. This is also why livestreaming or webinars are popular teaching tools. Interacting live with your audience builds instant rapport and trust.

Podcaster and internet personality Luria Petrucci released her first video to the world on December 23, 2005. Her show *Greek Brief* was one of the first video podcasts ever to exist. Just two months prior, Apple announced the release of their very first video iPod. Luria, who always had a fascination with technology, wanted to produce episodes for her new show before Christmas. Assuming people everywhere might be getting an Apple video iPod for Christmas, Luria wanted to seize the opportunity. At first, she wasn't fond of being on camera; she even used the alias "Cali Lewis" for her show. After recording her first episode, Luria called her mom and burst into tears. She was deathly afraid of what other people would think of her videos. However her passion for technology and for serving others pulled her through, and she got better over time.

Her courage to practice in public also brought her new opportunities. She was invited to cohost a new TV show in Canada and Australia entitled *Call for Help* with podcaster Leo Laporte. This proved to be a growth opportunity for Luria as she learned how to handle mistakes while she was live on-air. Each experience led to another growth opportunity. Next, Panasonic called to ask Luria to host a multiday livestreaming technology event that would be seen by thousands.

Today, Luria has spoken to live crowds of two thousand or more at in-person events and even appeared on major news outlets like CNN. Reflecting on her journey with video, she said, "I could have said 'NO' and could have stayed right where I was. But when someone asked me to do something, I said 'YES,' then just did it and ignored that loud voice inside saying I didn't know how!"[5] Most influencers I know didn't start out perfect on camera. They just got started. Each time they hit Record, their confidence grew. Being capable and comfortable on camera is a skill that can be learned. Now it's your turn to learn how to easily create content that never grows old.

You may be thinking, *How am I supposed to come up with all of this content?* Not only that, but, *How do I create content that doesn't become outdated only a few months later?* If that's you, pay special attention to what's coming up next. The secret to creating consistent content comes down to using three simple templates.

## Three Evergreen Content Templates

Over the last ten years as a content creator, I've lost count of how many blog posts, podcasts, and videos I've published. But what I do know is that all of them fall under three simple content templates.

Before we get into the templates, let's define what we mean by the word *evergreen*. The best type of content to create is content that will be as relevant, true, and helpful ten years from now as it is today. Like an evergreen tree that never changes regardless of the season, your content will keep on serving through the years.

Still to this day, my most visited page each month on my career coach blog is a blog post I published in 2011. It's a post offering advice about what to do if you've been on a job interview and you've heard nothing from the employer. The tips shared in that article are just as true and relevant today as they were in 2011. That's the power of creating content that lasts. You want your templates to inspire evergreen content. And that's exactly what these templates will do.

I've used these three templates over and over again to create fresh new content for my audience. They work well in writing for any format: blog posts, podcasts, or videos. You can deploy these templates in any niche or industry regardless of the audience. An easy way to remember these three content templates (and the purpose behind them) is to think about three "E" words: encourage, educate, and empower.

### Template 1: Encourage your audience through stories.

Stories are powerful. Stories and experiences from your life can be like windows that let the light in for your audience. It's one thing to offer teachings that add value to other people's lives; it's another thing to deliver those teachings through a story. One of the most life-impactful ways to teach a lesson is by telling a story. In his book *Lead with a Story*, author Paul Smith shares ten compelling reasons to tell stories:

1. Storytelling is simple.
2. Storytelling is timeless.
3. Stories are demographic-proof.
4. Stories are contagious.

5. Stories are easier to remember.

6. Stories inspire.

7. Stories appeal to all types of learners.

8. Stories fit better where most of the learning happens in the workplace.

9. Stories put the listener in a mental learning mode.

10. Telling stories shows respect for the audience.[6]

Don't forget that, in the context of a message-based business, the value of telling a story is to teach a lesson. Using stories in your content marketing is more than journaling about your life. There must be a lesson in your story that's worth sharing to make your story useful to the reader or listener. Paul Smith goes on to share his formula for telling good stories. To make a story memorable, he uses the acronym CAR.

- Context—What's the necessary background information for the story to make sense? Where and when did the story take place? Who is the main character? What did he or she want? What obstacles was he or she facing?
- Action—What did the main character do? What happened once the main character began taking action?
- Result—What happened to the main character in the end? What lessons did he or she learn that can apply to all of us?[7]

The story can come out of your own experience or the experience of someone you know, or it can come from something you've read. A story has two applications: First, you use it to open up your article, podcast, or video. Second, you use it to bring the article, podcast, or video to a conclusion by sharing ways to apply the lessons learned.

## The "Story" Content Template
## Your Catchy Headline

Open up the content by sharing your funny or interesting story in detail. (Introduction: two to four paragraphs)

*Lesson 1: State the first lesson (subheadline).*
Write one or two paragraphs applying lesson one.

*Lesson 2: State the second lesson (subheadline).*
Write one or two paragraphs applying lesson two.

*Lesson 3: State the third lesson (subheadline).*
Write one or two paragraphs applying lesson three.

Repeat this process for each step . . .

Write a conclusion paragraph and you are done!

### Template 2: Educate your audience through instructional content.

By instructional content, I'm referring to answering the "how-to" question. As we've already noted, people are not looking for information; they are looking for transformation. The best way to facilitate transformation is by creating practical, actionable content. Think steps, not information.

More often than not, such an article or podcast's headline will begin with "How to." Picture your audience sitting across from you and asking, "How?" Use the preposition "by" to answer their question. For example, if our topic is "How to Start a Car" our step-by-step outline might go something like this: "by grabbing the keys to the car, then unlocking the car, then placing the key in the ignition, then turning the ignition."

Obviously, this is an overly simplistic example, but you get the point. Using this "how to/by" strategy will help you create an outline for any type of content quickly. The goal with practical, actionable content is for your reader or listener to get an answer to a challenge and take a step forward. Any time you help someone achieve a result, you've won over a lifelong fan.

## The "How" Content Template
## Your Catchy Headline

Open up the blog post with a question, statement, short story, or illustration. (Introduction: one or two paragraphs)

**Step 1. Write the first step (subheadline).**

Write one or two paragraphs explaining step 1.

**Step 2: Write the second step (subheadline).**

Write one or two paragraphs explaining step 2.

**Step 3: Write the third step (subheadline).**

Write one or two paragraphs explaining step 3.

Repeat this process for each step . . .

Write a conclusion paragraph, and you are done!

### *Template 3: Empower your audience through inspirational content.*

Picture your audience sitting in front of you with their arms crossed. They are listening but a bit skeptical. The only way to influence them toward action is by answering the question "Why?" Why is exercising first thing in the morning better? Why should I reduce my use of social media before bedtime? Every niche audience will have its own particular "why" questions.

The best way to answer a "why" question is by creating a series of "because" statements. This naturally creates a persuasive outline for you. Think of your goal with this template as providing reasons why someone should change their perspective.

A few years ago, I wrote a blog article entitled *Five Reasons You Should Write an Amazon Kindle Book*. The goal of the article was to persuade and inspire my audience to self-publish a book on Amazon. The article does not go into how to publish a Kindle book.

That's a topic for another article. Someone must be convinced *why* they should do something before they care about the *how*. Using the "why" template, I came up with the following five reasons.

- because of the impressive sales statistics of Kindle books
- because you can benefit from Amazon's existing traffic
- because you can dramatically increase your brand awareness
- because you can provide amazing social proof to your audience
- because you can make some extra money each month writing about your passion

Once I had written a few paragraphs on each of the five reasons above, I had a blog post ready to go. Not only that, but I have a script written to turn my article into a podcast or video episode. Inspirational content helps to break down false beliefs your audience may have. It persuades them to change their perspective, and it motivates them toward action.

---

### The "Why" Content Template
### Your Catchy Headline

Begin your content with a question, statement, short story, or illustration. (Introduction: one or two paragraphs)

#### Point 1. Because . . . (subheadline).

Write one or two paragraphs explaining all the reasons why this point is important.

#### Point 2. Because . . . (subheadline).

Write one or two paragraphs explaining all the reasons why this point is important.

#### Point 3. Because . . . (subheadline).

Write one or two paragraphs explaining all the reasons why this point is important.

Repeat this process for each reason . . .

Write a conclusion paragraph and you are done!

---

All you need are three templates to create consistent content for your audience. Whether your desire is to blog, podcast, or record videos (or a combination of all three), these three templates will make your life easier.

But why should you be creating all of this content in the first place? Well, there are three big reasons. First, because content marketing is easier than self-promotion. Second, because it builds trust with your audience. Third, because it's one of the best ways to grow your email list. That's what we are going to talk about next.

# The Messenger Roadmap

## Create—What content type will you use to attract your audience?

We are now ready to complete another section of your Messenger Roadmap. While you could argue that there are more than three unique ways to create content, our goal here is to focus on the top three most effective methods.

Question: Which content type will you use first to attract your audience? Place a check mark next to, circle, or highlight your choice below.

- Blogging
- Podcasting
- Vlogging (Video Blogging)

Go to the Messenger Roadmap in the appendix and add your answer now.

# 13

## Capture

### *The Artful Exchange of Value for Email Addresses*

Can you tell a story in six seconds or less? That was the premise of a once-popular social media platform known as Vine. Twitter, known for keeping its messages short, acquired Vine in 2012 as a video-based platform with the same idea of brevity. Users had six seconds to tell their story via video. At its peak in 2016, Vine had well over a hundred million active users. That much daily activity created an opportunity for many previously unknown creatives. Some of these "superusers" amassed more than a million followers and became known as *Viners*. Then, the unthinkable happened. Without much warning, Twitter killed the platform. Sarah Austin, a writer for *Entrepreneur* magazine, wrote, "Almost overnight Twitter reduced Vine to little more than an archive of the world's shortest, most entertaining video content, leaving its survivors to abide on other platforms."[1]

Millions of followers gone overnight. Some Viners survived because they were already building a platform on YouTube, Facebook, and Instagram. But many others lost their fame and influence in an instant. It's a sad tale of what happens when we build our empire on rented land. Who knows if, in the days ahead, the same will happen to influencers on YouTube, Facebook, and Instagram. There is nothing wrong with leveraging these social ponds to attract our ideal audience. But smart messengers are ruthless about one crucial skill: *capturing an audience you own.*

## The Value of Having an Audience You Own

In this business, you can only take two things with you to the grave: your reputation and your email list. How you treat people while building your business determines your reputation. It's a critical component to building a business that lasts. But just as critical to your business is how you capture leads of potential customers. In fact I would go so far as to say that the energy and lifeblood of your message-based business is your email list.

Starting an email list is vital to controlling your financial destiny. If for some reason I lose access to my social media following, I will still be in business because I have an email list. I could send out a single email to my list, telling my followers where to find me next. With an email list, I have a business asset I own and traffic I can control at any time.

Will email always be around? We don't know what the future will hold, but for now email is the most dependable and effective way you have to reach your audience. Even if something better than email comes along, an email list will help you leverage the new tool to greater success. For the foreseeable future, building an email list is one of the smartest skills you can develop.

## Why You Need an Email List

Before we walk through some of my favorite strategies for building an email list, let's look in more detail at why having one is so vital to your success.

### 1. Your email list is the foundation of your business.

Remember the Hourglass Funnel I shared in chapter 11? The middle of the hourglass represents capturing emails in your business. The blog posts, podcasts, and videos you create should accomplish one primary purpose: attract people to get on your email list. Joining your email list should be the logical next step for anyone consuming your free content. You can attract your audience via search engines, social media, or paid advertising—three traffic options that we'll discuss further in chapter 15. But however you go about it, the goal should be to get them on your list. It's the foundation of your business.

### 2. Your email list is traffic you can control.

The office supply store Staples ran a TV commercial for the 2005 Super Bowl that became an instant hit. The concept was simple. It was about a bright red button, known as the Easy Button. Anytime you faced something challenging, all you had to do was hit the Easy Button and your problem was solved.

When I first started teaching others how to build a business online, I used to say there is no Easy Button to push. Building a business indeed takes time, energy, and effort. But on further reflection, I've come to the conclusion that there is an Easy Button after all. Once you press it, you can initiate instant traffic to your blog posts, podcasts, videos, webinars, and sales pages. It's called the Send button.

Want people to read your latest blog post? Send an email to your list. Want to make sales on a new online course you've created? Send an email. Want to host a webinar with thousands of live attendees? Send an email. Your email list equals traffic, and owning that list means you can control that traffic. That's why owning an email list is the most critical tool in your toolbox.

### 3. Your email list is the best way to make money in your business.

Time and time again, studies have been conducted to determine which method is the best at converting prospects into customers. Every time methods are tested, email marketing comes out on top. Hubspot, a customer software company, reports that email generates thirty-eight dollars for every dollar spent. If you're wondering whether people are still paying attention to email, consider this fact: 99 percent of consumers check their email every day. Of course that doesn't mean 99 percent of your email list will see or even open your emails. But the point is that the value of email doesn't appear to be changing anytime soon. The study also found 73 percent of millennials prefer communications from businesses to come via email.[2] The best tool in your business toolbox for making sales is your email list.

### 4. Your email list gives you instant access to your audience.

If you need to get the word out fast to your audience, which tool is the best to use? While some might say social media, think again. In 2015 Facebook upset many Facebook Fan Page owners by showing fewer Facebook posts to their fans. A Facebook Fan Page is a free tool any business can create to attract and communicate with their fans on Facebook. In times past, a new post would show up in the news feed to people who liked a business's page. Because of this, many marketers and influencers encouraged people to like their page. But once Facebook made adjustments to their algorithm, which ranks posts in users' news feeds, only 15 percent of fans saw posts from their favorite fan pages show up in their feed. While it's easy to be upset with Facebook, it is their traffic and their website to manage as they like. But when you own an email list, you aren't at the mercy of other platforms. If you want to get the attention of your audience, just send them an email.

### 5. The relationship is in the list.

Believe it or not, an email list is one of the most personal and intimate forms of communication you can own. I'm adamant about crafting personal emails in my business. I intentionally avoid fancy newsletter templates, logo headers, and footers. I want the email to feel like I only sent it to you. In fact, I've worked so hard at making my communication feel personal, my wife has replied to my emails asking if the email was just for her.

By making your emails personal, you make room for a relationship to develop. While your competition is pounding their list with only sales emails, you are opening a conversation. There's a saying in the online marketing community that I dislike: "The money is in the list." While technically accurate, it's the wrong focus. Focusing on money will get you a sale; focusing on the relationship will gain you a lifelong customer. The relationship is in the list. You must add value to your potential customer first. You do this by focusing on your relationship with the people on your list.

### 6. The money is in the relationship.

The money part comes more naturally if you've focused on the relationship first. The goal is not to manipulate a false relationship to get money. People see through that. The goal is to build genuine relationships through which you add value and have impact in people's lives, with income being a natural by-product of that.

Some messengers I meet struggle with the making money component of building a business. A common statement I hear is "I just want to serve people and get my story out to as many people as possible." For some people, making money feels like they've compromised on their intended mission. If you feel that tension, I have a simple exercise for you: write a list of all the influencers, speakers, writers, and coaches you admire. Next ask yourself this question: "How do they financially support their cause or mission?" The answer is money.

Money is not the root of all evil. *The love of money* is the root of all evil. The idea behind money being the root of all evil is an often misquoted verse that comes from the Bible.[3] It's not money itself, but it's the craving for money at the expense of others that makes it dangerous. Money itself is neutral, meaning it's not good or bad by default. It's your relationship to money that matters.

What if we viewed money as just a tool to make a greater impact on our mission? The formula is simple: Impact creates income, and income makes room for us to create more impact. Let me explain by way of example.

Writing a book is no easy feat. It's a commitment of hours upon hours of work. Once the writer is finished with the manuscript, it can be up to nine to twelve months before the book hits the shelf. What then allows authors like me the freedom to spend hours writing a book? The answer is the income we are already generating in our business. Income brings freedom; freedom gives space for more impact. It's a never-ending, ever-expanding cycle of influence.

Jeff Walker, in his bestselling book, *Launch*, states, "Having an email list is the closest thing you can have to a printing press that will print money for you."[4] Jeff goes on to share a particularly expensive time of his life when his family decided to move to

Colorado. They found a dream home but were short on the down payment they needed to get the property. That's when Jeff asked himself, *What type of offer can I create for my email list to raise that amount of money quickly?* From there he offered a special sale to the people on his list, which helped him generate the $70,000 he needed to acquire his dream home. That's the power of owning an email list. You're able to generate sales from people who want what you have to offer, people you already have a relationship with.

## How to Build an Email List Fast

The good news is that you only need to answer three basic questions to be successful at building an email list:

1. Who do you want to attract?
2. Where can you find them?
3. What tool will you use to attract them?

### *1. Who do you want to attract?*

Before you jump into choosing tools, methods, and strategies, you must answer a fundamental question first: Who do you want to attract? Since we covered this subject in depth back in chapter 8, answering this question should be fairly easy. You'll find it right there on your Messenger Roadmap. But identifying your audience is only one part of the formula. You also need to know where they are hanging out.

### *2. Where can you find them?*

How do I find my audience? This is a question I hear frequently. The answer is to go where your audience—the theoretical fish you're fishing for—is already congregating. If you are unsure of where that is at the moment, that's okay. A great place to start is by exploring these three ponds (or traffic sources):

- Free—ponds anyone can access (search engines and social media)
- Paid—ponds you need to pay to get access (paid advertising)
- Partner—ponds your friends own (affiliate relationships and guest contributions)

In chapter 15 we will do a deep dive into these three traffic sources. I'll even share with you several traffic strategies you can use that fall under each of the three "traffic ponds" mentioned above. By the time we are done, you'll know exactly where your audience is congregating.

### 3. What tool will you use to attract them?

In order to get your potential audience interested in your message, you must create something of value. As we established earlier, building an email list is the artful exchange of value for email addresses. What can you create that is so valuable that your audience will be willing to give you their email address? Don't make the mistake of falling into the "join my newsletter" trap. This is an easy mistake many new online creators make. They launch a website, hear the importance of building an email list, and add a "join my newsletter" option. It doesn't work anymore. People are a bit more protective of their email addresses, and rightly so. But if you offer for free something they would have paid for, they will gladly give you their email address.

I've tried every method I could find to build my email list over the years. Some were successful, and some were not. In time, I learned that several list-building methods brought me great success, and I've used them over and over again. Here are my top nine:

- *Content Upgrade*—Create bonus content for your blog posts, podcasts, and videos that your followers can access by subscribing to your email list. Think about it. If they are reading your blog posts, they already have an interest in that topic. Doesn't it make sense to offer bonus content in exchange for an email address? An example of one that's worked well for me is to offer a PDF checklist related to the blog post that the reader can access by giving you their email address.

- *Contest Giveaway*—Host a free contest giveaway. People love entering for a chance to win something for free. Include free access to online courses you've created or even give away a collection of your favorite books your audience would enjoy. A giveaway package that has worked well for me is a bundle of some of my online courses.

- *Five-Day Challenge*—Design a free multiday email course. People love mini-challenges, especially if it helps them accomplish one of their goals. It's also a great way to provide free value at the beginning of a relationship. A popular challenge I created was called the 5-Day Launch Your Blog Challenge. Each day for five days the subscriber received an email with a link to a video tutorial on how to create a blog.

- *PDF Blueprint*—Take a popular topic in your niche and create a helpful mind map. A mind map is a visual tool used to organize information on a given topic. You can also simply turn your blog post into a PDF that someone can download in exchange for an email address. One of our most popular blueprints is called the Discover Your Message Blueprint. It's a nine-page PDF the subscriber can use to narrow down their audience ideas to a specific niche.

- *Quiz*—People love self-discovery. Design a quiz or assessment that shares with them an insightful result. After they complete the quiz, they put in their email address to see their results. Remember the thirty-two-question Influencer Voice Assessment from chapter 7? I created an online version of the assessment that compiles your results for you. You can see it in action at YourMessageMattersBook.com /quiz.

- *Webinar*—If you have a teacher's heart, you'll love webinars. Create a free online workshop on a compelling topic. Offer free access to anyone who registers. The attendee learns from you in a live environment and it builds value and trust.

- *Testimonial*— Purchase an online course or coaching program from an influencer. Implement the training and share with them your results. Influencers are always looking for case studies and testimonials. While maybe not a direct list-building strategy, it's an effective promotion strategy. I'm surprised more people do not do it.

- *Virtual Summit*—Host an online conference. Interview fifteen influencers, authors, and speakers in your niche and then invite them to promote your free virtual summit to their email lists. As attendees register for your free virtual summit, you build your email list.

- *Affiliate Product Launch*—If you already have an online course, consider inviting other influencers to promote your course to their list. A great way to get started is to create a PDF blueprint or webinar and have them share it to their list. You will both build your list and boost your sales.

You don't need to implement all nine list-building strategies to be effective, though you could if you wanted to. Executing just one in a focused way can lead to amazing results.

Would you like some step-by-step instructions on how to do each of the above? I've created a blueprint for each list-building method that you can download for free. We keep these blueprints updated so you can be certain you have the latest tips and tools to build your business. Just go to YourMessageMattersBook.com/tools.

## How a High School Teacher Added 1,365 Emails in One Week

Cory Peppler, a public school teacher by day, had a passion for helping parents manage their teens in a digital world. After learning the power of a virtual summit to build one's audience, he decided to use this strategy. For months he performed research on who to invite and what tools he should use to pull his summit off. But over time his diligent research was turning into procrastination. The fear of rejection and the thought that he was wasting his time began to dominate his thinking. But I had just the idea to help him get unstuck.

Every year I host a two-day live event designed to help messengers build their businesses. I knew Cory would be attending, and I asked him ahead of time if he'd be open to doing a live coaching session with me onstage. He agreed. While onstage, Cory began to share all of the research, preparation, and legwork he had done. But then he admitted two things:

1. He had no deadline for the virtual summit.
2. He had not even invited the first guest expert.

He had compiled a list of one hundred influencers he wanted to invite. He had even crafted emails he wanted to send them. But doubt, distraction, and fear had held him back from pushing

Send. Even the audience members at my live event began to speak up and encourage him just to hit Send. It was just the nudge Cory needed. Within sixty days of the live event, Cory hosted his Digital Parenting Summit. By executing the virtual summit blueprint we shared earlier, within one week his list grew from 165 subscribers to over 1,500. He also decided to sell recordings of his interviews with experts from the summit. By the time the event was over, Cory made an additional $1,500. Not only that, but he now had something to sell his audience in the months and weeks to come. This was the first real income his business had generated.

Capturing leads is essential to your message-based business. Once someone is on your list, you can begin to build that relationship. As the relationship grows, your audience will start to know, like, and trust you. The logical next step in the relationship will be for them to purchase the products and services you've created. That's where we're going next.

# The Messenger Roadmap

## Capture—What tool will you use to capture leads?

Let's start building that email list of yours. The goal is not to implement all nine of these strategies at once. For now, I would like you to just pick one that you'll implement first.

Question: What tool will you use first to capture leads?

- Content Upgrade
- Contest Giveaway
- Five-Day Challenge
- PDF Blueprint
- Quiz
- Webinar
- Testimonial
- Virtual Summit
- Affiliate Product Launch

Don't forget to add your choice to the Messenger Roadmap in the appendix in the back of the book. Also, if you'd like to get free access to my up-to-date list-building blueprints on how to do each of the nine above, go to YourMessageMattersBook.com/tools.

# 14

# Compile

## *Package Your Knowledge into Products and Services*

It all started with a Sunday school class. Dan Miller wasn't looking to become a coach, speaker, or writer. He was already a successful entrepreneur who owned multiple businesses. But he saw a need to help people in his church who were in career transition. Each Sunday he taught others how to find more meaningful work. This was a fairly cutting-edge approach to the traditional Sunday school model. Before too long, people from other churches and even other cities began to attend this weekly session. In an effort to accommodate more people, Dan eventually turned it into a free Monday night seminar, which he ran for over eight years.

The more questions people asked in his class, the more products Dan began creating. He compiled his teaching into a three-ring binder that could be purchased even by people who didn't attend his weekly sessions. Out of curiosity he built a website and began to post some of his products for sale online, and to his surprise they began to sell. That's when Dan discovered he had a gold mine.

He asked himself, *How many different ways can I repurpose this message into products and services?* It turned out that his answer was a lot. Over the next few years, Dan expanded on his core message and launched a number of products, including (but not limited to) the following:

- *48 Days to the Work You Love* book (*New York Times* bestseller)
- *48 Days to the Work You Love Workbook*
- 48 Days to the Work You Love online seminar
- 48 Days mastery coaching certification
- 48 Days Mastermind
- 48 Days personal coaching
- 48 Days Eagles (monthly membership site)
- 48 Days yearly cruise[1]

What started out as a Sunday school class has grown into a message-based business with multiple income streams. That's the power of constructing many products and services out of one message.

## The Messenger's Product Map Defined

As seen in Dan Miller's example, there are multiple ways to create income with your message. In this chapter, I'll walk you through twelve different revenue streams you can build no matter what niche you serve (see the figure below). Each is a potential gold mine. You can make a living by just creating one, but you can make a fortune by incorporating all twelve. Most people have no idea how to monetize their message. The answer is found in applying the Messenger Product Map. I can tell you how.

14.1

## The Messenger Product Map Defined

| Type of Influencer | Beginner | Intermediate | Advanced |
|---|---|---|---|
| Writer | Publish a Kindle Book | Publish a Physical Book | Record an Audiobook |
| Teacher | Host a Paid Webinar Series | Create an Online Course | Launch a Membership Site |
| Speaker | Publish a Speaking Page | Host a High-End Workshop | Host a Large Live Event |
| Coach | Publish a "Work with Me" Page | Launch a 4–6 Week Group Coaching Experience | Launch a High-End 1-Year Mentoring or Mastermind Group |

## Writing Income Streams

Getting paid to write. Many people desire to do this, but they struggle. "According to writer Joseph Epstein, '81 percent of Americans feel that they have a book in them—and should write it.'"[2] That's over 200 million people. And yet only a small percentage ever do it. An even smaller percentage will go on to publish their work and share it with the world. We could assume this is because publishing companies are careful and precise as to what book projects they take on, but there is no publisher's approval needed to self-publish.

Upfront costs don't even have to play a significant role in getting your message out to the world. Before the dawn of the internet, self-publishing was a costly and risky adventure. To work with a self-publishing house, an author had to purchase several thousand copies of their own book upfront. After they received their shipment, they had to figure out how to sell and ship their books to their readers. That's a lot of work for a twenty-dollar product.

The good news is that the process is much simpler today. In the case of a digital book, zero fulfillment is needed. Meaning when someone purchases your book, it is delivered to them instantly. You even have the opportunity to freely display your book for sale on high-traffic sites like Amazon. Even with physical books, the process has become much simpler. Once a physical book is up for sale on Amazon, there is zero responsibility for you in storing inventory, fulfilling orders, or handling customer service. After the purchase is made, Amazon handles the rest. Then monthly, you receive a commission check in your bank account. While there are many ways to earn money with writing, we are going to focus on three: digital book, physical book, and audiobook.

*Publish a digital book.* Also known as an ebook, a digital book is a self-published book you sell online. Originally, most ebooks were sold on the author's website. Today, there are several popular websites where you can sell your self-published book. Writing and publishing a digital book is not a difficult process. Just follow these five steps:

1. Write the first draft of your book.
2. Edit and format your book (or hire an editor).
3. Get a digital book cover design.
4. Upload your book and cover design.
5. Set your price and publish your book.

*Publish a physical book*. Being able to publish a book in a physical form that you can hold is also easier than ever before. If you've already published an ebook, doesn't it make sense to also turn your project into a physical book? You've already done the hard work of writing the manuscript. It's just the matter of re-purposing your work into a physical format. There are two parts to a physical book that need to be created:

- the interior design
- the front and back cover

You'll be better off outsourcing these two pieces of your project. First, find an affordable contractor via a freelancing service online to create the interior design and format of your book. While you could do it yourself through online video tutorials, spending the money to have someone do it for you will give you back more time to do other things for your business.

The second step to outsource is the design of your cover. This task is a bit more complicated for a physical book than it is for a digital one. The page length of your book determines the size of the spine. For example, if your book is two hundred pages long, you'll have a big enough book spine to list the title and author of the book on the spine itself. A designer can help you to get this right.

If you already have your book available as a digital book, is it worth the trouble to make it a physical book? The short answer is yes. With my first self-published book, people purchased it in all three formats: digital, physical, and audiobook. Some of your followers will prefer a certain format. To my surprise, I had many followers who preferred only the audiobook version. I would have missed out on revenue by not repurposing my content into an audiobook.

*Record an audiobook*. Audiobook sales have been growing over the years and are now a multibillion-dollar-a-year business. You can take advantage of this opportunity. Using free audio recording software and a quality mic, you can turn your master bedroom closet into a makeshift recording studio. How do I know? That's the exact process I used in recording my first audiobook.

One Saturday when my family was out of town I seized on the opportunity to record my entire audiobook. I set up my makeshift studio in the master bedroom closet among all the hanging clothes. I did this to make a soundproof room and to improve the acoustics of my recording. Over the next few hours, I read and recorded one chapter at a time. While it did take a few hours to record the whole book, I was done with the work in a single day. From there, I uploaded the recordings of each chapter and submitted my project on Amazon. Other than promoting the audiobook, my work was done. Every single month for the last five years, I've received commission checks for the work I did that one Saturday morning. That's called leverage. Every business opportunity that can result in ongoing income is a point that you can leverage. The more you invest in leverage points in your business, the more freedom you will gain over time. Are you beginning to see how your message can grow in both impact and income?

## Teacher Income Streams

Teacher income streams include anything that can be defined as a one-to-many product. With this type of income stream, you can sell the exact same product to as many people as possible. This allows you to make money whether you are working or not. If you have a teacher's heart, then you'll love the income streams we discuss here.

As a former high school teacher, I enjoyed tackling a topic with a group of students. But what I wasn't excited about was the context. The rigorous daily schedule and the classroom management drained me. Perhaps you've had the same experience, or maybe you have avoided teaching because you felt similar concerns. But what if you could get all the upsides of teaching without any of the downsides? Well, it is possible. Let me show you how.

*Host a paid webinar series.* Think of a webinar as an online class. As the teacher of that class, it's your job to put together the presentation slides and invite people to attend. The people who attend do so in the comfort of their own home without having to travel. As long as they have access to a laptop with an internet connection, they can attend.

If you've been to a webinar like this, it was probably for free. Free webinars can be a great way for you as an influencer to build a list of leads fast. But you can also sell access to your webinars. All you need is a sales page and an order button to get started. From there, you will create a deadline and host a series of webinars with the paid attendees based on your schedule.

*Create an online course.* An online course and a paid webinar series might sound the same, but they are different. With a paid webinar series, you are teaching your material to a live audience in a four-to-six-week time frame. In most cases with an online course, you are recording step-by-step video tutorials and selling them after the fact.

Is creating an online course worth the effort? As mentioned before, having an online course to sell is leveraged income. Think about it. Once you've created the course, you can sell it over and over again without having to do anything else related to it. Selling an online course is one of the fastest ways out of the trading-time-for-dollars trap. You can package your knowledge and advice into recorded videos that people can access at any time. Meanwhile, you are spending your valuable time on other revenue-generating activities.

*Launch a membership site.* What's even better than leveraged income? Recurring income. One of the best ways to get it is to have a membership site: essentially, a "gated" part of your website filled with content that can be accessed only by members who pay monthly for the privilege. Having a membership site brings recurring revenue into your business each and every month. You sell your membership site once and then get paid over and over again for permission to get access to it. This is a great income stream for teachers. If you have a teacher's heart, you will love running a membership site.

Let me give you an example. For the past eight years, I've run a membership site called the Online Business Fast Track Lab. Besides access to the vault of past recorded classes, members get two live trainings with me each month.

At the beginning of the month I host a live members-only training called Fast Track Class. It's a sixty-minute live video class where I teach how to implement something I do in my business. Members get to ask questions and get feedback in real time. At the end of the month I host a one-hour live Office Hours call. Members can submit any questions they have about growing an online business. We call it popcorn-style learning. It's a little bit of this and a little bit of that, but a whole lot of fun. We cover a wide range of topics and tools during that one hour.

If you love to teach, you'll love running a membership site. But unlike a traditional teaching job, you only need to show up two hours a month to teach (using my example above)! Also, you get to use your own creativity and experience to come up with new class ideas each month.

## Speaking Income Streams

Getting paid to speak. Maybe this is a dream of yours: to be onstage in front of hundreds or even thousands and sharing your passion with a live audience. Getting paid to speak is not just a privilege reserved for the super famous. Event planners across every industry are constantly in need of good speakers. Do a quick search online for "your topic + conference" or "your topic + event." What you find may surprise you. There may be more people, gathering in more places, to talk about your subject matter than you realized. Besides being a valuable income stream in itself, speaking can also open the pathway for you to sell all of the other products you are creating. At events, you can have a speaker's table where you sell your books, courses, coaching, and more.

What if you don't want to be a road warrior? A limiting belief I had for years was that I didn't want to be on the road all of the time and spend that much time away from family. What I failed to understand is getting paid to speak is not all or nothing. You can decide to limit your speaking to three or four times a year, focusing on the events that give you the most leverage.

*Publish a speaking page.* While it might not generate speaking requests overnight, one of the first essential steps of an aspiring speaker is to publish a speaking page. Create a page on your website to let event planners know you're a speaker who is available and open for business.

*Host a high-end workshop.* There is nothing quite like getting to be face-to-face with your audience. The thrill of sharing, teaching, and serving others in person can be exhilarating.

One of the reasons most influencers steer away from in-person events is because of the fear of logistics. Since they don't have an event planning background, the fear of unknown costs and event details holds them back. Even worse, they wonder, *What if I go to all the trouble of planning an event and not enough people attend?* I know these are real challenges that most influencers face because those were my fears and questions too. For me, the answer was to produce a limited high-end workshop. Event planning becomes easier when you are managing fewer than ten people. The benefit to the attendees is they get more personalized attention from you.

It's a small, yet intimate setting. One where real breakthroughs can happen. What you wish you could do for many someday, you can do now with a few. The joy of going deep with a handful of people can be transformational—for them and for you. To make hosting a high-end limited workshop worth your time and attention, you will need to charge a premium rate.

*Host a large in-person event.* This is an advanced income strategy that makes more sense to tackle as your platform grows, but it can be incredibly rewarding when you're ready. While people attend in part because they want to learn from you, there's a bigger benefit for the attendee. That's being in a room with passionate like-minded people who are heading in the same direction. As the attendees share stories, failures, and successes, they begin to bond with one another.

While it's hard to define a large event, I think of it as anything with over fifty people in attendance. Anything under that I would call a workshop. Once you go over fifty people, more logistics and planning are required. For example, a microphone and AV equipment must be secured so everyone in the room can easily hear you. Sure, an event takes some work, but the effort is worth it. There's nothing like teaching people in a live, in-person setting.

## Coaching Income Streams

A common question I hear from creative entrepreneurs goes something like this: "I've been working on my business for a while. Why am I not making any money?" My response comes in the form of a question: "If I were to go to your website right now with a payment method in hand, could I buy something from you?" The answer I get most of the time is "Not yet." They are still working on the online course, membership site, or book. The hard truth is that you're not open for business until you have something to sell.

One of the fastest ways to open for business is to offer coaching services. When I launched my career advice blog for accounting professionals, coaching was my first source of income. All it required was that I set up a "Work with me" page and include a coaching-services Order button.

*Publish a "Work with me" page.* You can open your business over a single weekend simply by publishing a "Work with me" page on your website. As people begin to consume your blog posts, podcasts, and videos, they will naturally want you to personally coach them. All that is required to get started is a payment method and a way to schedule a time slot on your calendar. Making money sharing your advice and experiences is one of the easiest ways to get started.

But what if you doubt that anyone would pay you for your advice? In a recent article, Sia Mohajer shared what he calls "the 3 Book Rule." If you've read just three books on a topic, then you know more about it than 99 percent of the population.[3] Launching a "Work with me" page is one of the fastest ways to open for business.

*Launch a four-to-six-week group-coaching experience.* The fastest way for you to scale your coaching practice is to launch a group coaching experience. Consider the possibilities. If you are coaching ten individuals on a weekly basis, that's ten different appointments on your calendar. But what if you could get all ten clients to show up on a call at the same time? How many hours would that free up for you? Now, before you think your clients would never agree to that, consider this. People grow best in community. The power of group coaching comes from people sharing their similar challenges and frustrations with one another in a group setting.

*Launch a high-end one-year paid mastermind group.* Every coach should consider launching a one-year high-end mastermind group. It's a more exclusive opportunity that comes at a premium price.

Most of the time the group is capped at a certain size. Members of your mastermind group typically will get more access to you. Of course, you can set what those parameters are. Another way to picture how this type of group can work is to think about mentoring. By joining your exclusive group, the members get regular, ongoing mentoring from you. This is attractive for potential prospects because learning directly from you gives them the opportunity to get further faster in their business.

## How I Created Seven Perpetual Income Streams in Twelve Months from One Message

What if I told you there was a smarter and better way to get your message out to the masses in half the time? For many bloggers, authors, speakers, and content creators, it's hard to see the big picture. We often get locked into the next promotion we think will catapult our business profits only to become disappointed when our single product doesn't get the attention we think it deserves.

The answer is to repurpose.

Smart messengers take their *single core message* and repurpose it into many different products. They are not dependent on just one avenue for sharing their message but instead have many entry points for customers and several pathways for reaching their tribe. How would your life be different twelve months from now if you had seven different perpetual income streams coming into your business all from a single message? That's what amplifying your message can do.

The idea came to me one day in a Panera Bread restaurant. One of my coaching clients had driven over two and a half hours to spend two hours with me in person. As he was describing his dilemma to me, an idea popped into my head.

"It sounds like you need to design an expert's product wheel," I said. I then pulled out a napkin and drew out the diagram you see below.

14.2
## Hub and Spoke Blueprint

Today I call it the Hub and Spoke Blueprint. Since that day, I've taught this same blueprint to thousands of speakers, teachers, writers, and coaches. At the center of the wheel is your core message. Each of the outside circles represents a product or service you offer related to your core message. As you can see, there are multiple ways you can get paid to deliver the same message.

This blueprint is simple in design, but I've found it to be a very powerful way to help others customize their business income plans to utilize their strengths.

Have you ever shared advice with someone else while at the same time thinking you too needed to heed the advice? I certainly have, and I left the coaching meeting that day knowing very well that I needed to do the exact same thing I had told my client to do. At the time I was working on my next book concept. I was looking for a way to create products and revenue streams beyond the new book itself. That's when I decided to commit the next twelve months to creating seven income streams around the single message of the book I was planning.

Here's the exact twelve-month timeline I followed.

- Month 1. Created the basic outline (or success steps) for my message.
- Months 2–4. Wrote the draft of my book.
- Month 5. Released the Kindle version of my book (income stream 1).
- Month 6. Released the self-published paperback version of my book (income stream 2).
- Month 7. Released the audiobook version on Amazon, iTunes, and Audible (income stream 3).
- Month 8. Wrote three keynote talks from the book (income stream 4).
- Month 9. Launched a new membership site (income stream 5).
- Month 10. Launched a group coaching program (income stream 6).
- Month 12. Hosted a live, in-person, high-end workshop (income stream 7).

## How to Earn $150,000 Next Year with Your Message

I would like to get extremely practical for you now. Before you finish this book, I want you to have a concrete plan for how to grow your business over the next twelve months. To begin, it's important for you to understand that there are three ways to grow a business.

1. *Activate*—Expand your customer base with a low-end product (under $50).

2. *Subscribe*—Sustain your business with recurring revenue ($30–$1,000 or more a month).

3. *Monetize*—Grow profits with higher-ticket offers ($1,000–$5,000 or more).

*Activate.* First you need a low-end offer to help expand your customer base. Ideally, this should be a digital product under fifty dollars. The goal of activation is to convert a prospect on your list to a buyer. The goal of the sale is not profit but expansion of your customer base. When someone purchases something from you, the relationship fundamentally changes. To put it another way, they move from being a fan to a follower. A lower-priced product is the logical first step in this shift. Examples of products that can activate your prospects to action include books, audiobooks, mini online courses, flash sales, or single coaching sessions.

*Subscribe.* Nothing will sustain your business and message like recurring revenue. To make it even easier, we are now living in the subscription economy. More and more people prefer to purchase products and services on a monthly recurring basis. Building a subscription model into your business is one of the smartest moves you can make. You sell once and get paid over and over again.

As mentioned earlier, I've been the owner of a membership site for over eight years. I still have monthly paying customers who signed up from my initial launch all those many years ago. If you serve people well, they will stick around. They begin to see you as their long-term mentor who can help them get to where they want to go. Other examples of recurring revenue include software, monthly recurring affiliate programs, monthly coaching services, and any other monthly service you provide. Adding a subscription model to your message-based business will go a long way to helping you maintain your monthly cash flow.

*Monetize.* This at last is the point where the real profit begins to flow into your business. Your first step, the low-end offer, has turned a lead into a customer. The next step, the subscription offer, has given you recurring business operating capital. Now the high-end offer will bring profit into your business.

One of my mentors once told me, "There will always be a percentage of your audience who would buy something more from you if you had it available." You may only convert 1 to 5 percent of your audience on your higher-end products, but having a product or service that you can sell in this higher price range is essential to growing your business.

The price point of a high-end offer varies widely from industry to industry. For the sake of keeping things simple, let's label anything above a $1,000 investment as a high-end offer. Do you have a product or service that you could sell for $1,000 or more? If not, you should create one.

Offering a product or service in the thousands of dollars might be difficult for you to imagine. I get that. I was that way too when I first started out. My first high-end offer back in 2009 was thirty days of career coaching for $1,200. I often wondered if anyone would ever pay that. To my surprise, people did. Not only that, but it wasn't long before I realized I was undercharging what I was worth.

The important thing is to just start somewhere. In addition to one-on-one coaching, a few other examples of high-end products include giving keynote talks, coaching groups, or serving as a one-year mastermind. We went into more depth on each of these earlier in this chapter.

Now that you understand the three ways to grow a business, let's look at an example you can use when creating your own plan:

- *Activate*—Selling just three low-cost courses per day at $50 each will earn you $4,200 a month, or $50,400 a year.
- *Subscribe*—Enrolling just 150 people into a $30 per month membership site will earn you $4,500 a month, or $54,000 a year.

- *Monetize*—Enrolling just 10 people into your high-ticket mastermind group at $5,000 will earn you $50,000 a year.

Using just three of the twelve income strategies we've discussed, we've found a way to generate $154,400 a year. Even if you were only half as successful as we predicted with the numbers above, that would be enough for most people to quit their day job. How could life be different for you over the next year if you were to implement a plan like this?

## What about the Traffic Problem?

As you may have already noticed, there's still one essential element we need to make all of this work: traffic. The fourth habit of our Hourglass Funnel is the connect habit, and that's the last piece we need to bring our plan together. This final habit will help you discover how you can best connect with people and peers to get noticed and heard. It's through this process that people enter into our world and move through our process of creating (giving value), capturing (building leads), and compiling (earning revenue). Let's get started!

# The Messenger Roadmap

## Compile—What will you sell to help your audience?

Nice work! You now know over twelve different ways to earn money with your message. While I'm sure you want all twelve products to be created in the next thirty days, it's not practical. Instead, my goal for you is to pick the first income stream you will create and then take the steps you need to do in order to officially be "open for business." Here are the two steps I recommend you take:

Step 1. *Write down your primary influencer voice*. Remember the Influencer Voice Assessment you took in chapter 7? The test should have revealed to you whether your primary influencer voice is teacher, writer, speaker, or coach. Go review your answer and record it here:

My primary influencer voice is: _____.

Step 2. *Choose one income method that's in alignment with your primary influencer voice*. I believe your fastest path to income and impact is to lean into your primary influencer voice first. My recommendation is that you choose a product to create that matches your voice.

Let me be clear. It's totally okay to choose one that doesn't match your voice if you prefer. Eventually, you should capitalize on all twelve income streams if possible. Choosing one that matches your primary influencer voice is simply more likely to set you up for success. Pick one from the list below and then add it to your Messenger Roadmap in the appendix. Awesome! Now let's start getting you some traffic!

**Writer Income Streams**
- publish a digital book
- publish a physical book
- record an audiobook

**Teacher Income Streams**
- host a paid webinar series
- create an online course
- launch a membership site

**Speaker Income Streams**
- publish a speaking page
- host a high-end workshop
- host a large, in-person event

**Coaching Income Streams**
- publish a "Work with me" page
- launch a four-to-six-week group-coaching experience
- launch a high-end, one-year mastermind group

# 15

# Connect

## *How to Attract Your Audience to Your Message*

When I first met Joseph Nicoletti, he was a corporate employee by day and side hustler by night. His deepest desire was to carve out some influence online and build a business he could run from home. One day his opportunity came.

While paying attention to the conversation happening on Twitter and elsewhere, Joseph noticed a pain point many writers were experiencing. They struggled with how to use Scrivener to write their books. Scrivener is a popular book-writing software many famous authors use and many nonfamous ones too. The problem was that the program didn't come with much instruction on how to use the software. Many aspiring writers bought the software but then had no idea how to use it.

In their frustration, Joseph recognized an opportunity. He created an entire step-by-step video course on how to use Scrivener. But he didn't have much of an audience to sell his course. That's when Joseph decided to build partner relationships. I like to refer to it as "partner traffic." Who already has a following and email list that you can partner with in order to build your list? That's exactly what Joseph started doing.

He began by creating a list of influencers who talk about writing books. Some of them were known in the fiction space; others were focused on nonfiction. Once he compiled a list of potential partners, he reached out to them. Most of them were already teaching about how to write a book, but not how to use Scrivener. He offered to host a free webinar to their audiences on how to use Scrivener. At the end of each training, he would then offer his course for sale. For any purchases of his course made as a result, he would split the revenue 50/50 with the partner. This was a winning scenario for both parties.

Since Joseph was hosting the webinar, he was able to grow his email list by the hundreds (if not thousands) with each webinar. He also earned revenue for his business with each course sale he made. His partners delivered the traffic; Joseph brought the traffic a paid solution to their problem.

In a little over a year, Joseph had built his email list to over twenty-five thousand subscribers. He made enough sales off his course and added enough people to his email list to transition out of his day job into his own business.[1] That's the power of tapping into a traffic strategy. When it comes to traffic, there are only three types: free, paid, and partner. In this chapter you'll learn how to maximize your results by implementing these three proven traffic strategies.

## Free Traffic: Search, Social, and Subscriber

Growing up in the Midwest, I spent many summers in the country. My grandparents owned a piece of land in northern Indiana. One day while my family and I were visiting, I came across an old-fashioned water pump on the property. Not knowing how it worked, I asked my grandfather for help.

He said, "You have to manually pump the handle over and over again for several minutes until the water comes out." I grabbed the handle and started pumping away. After thirty seconds of effort, I got tired and quit.

"No," said my grandpa, "You can't give up that easy. Keep going." Since my arm was already tired, I tried using my other arm. After another thirty seconds or so, to my surprise, water came out. I stopped pumping the handle, and the water stopped.

"You have to keep pumping son, but the good news is that once the water starts, you don't have to pump as hard. You can ease up and let it flow," said Grandpa. I'll never forget that day because I did something that felt difficult, but I kept going and succeeded.

Every messenger's ultimate dream is to have loads of free traffic flowing to their site daily. But it's not as easy as "If you write it, they will come." Sources of free traffic are much like the old water pump. You won't see immediate results from them, but disciplined action over time will lead to free traffic flowing to your site. Investing that time today will lead to great results later. I've been working at this for ten years. Now every day, whether I'm working or not, thousands of new visitors come to my site via past content I've created.

When it comes to free traffic, there are three strategies: search, social, and subscriber. Each of these sources takes time to build up, but once you've done it, consistently adding new leads to your business becomes easier.

### Free Traffic Source 1: Search Traffic

The goal is for your website to show up in the list of results people get when they do an online search. Search traffic originates anywhere a web search user is seeking information, ideas, or answers online.

This is where you have an advantage over every other business out there. By regularly publishing helpful blog posts, podcasts, and videos, you'll have a greater chance of showing up in the search engines. While people pay for ads to show up in search results, wouldn't you rather show up there for free? By creating keyword-rich content (also known as blog posts), you'll give yourself a greater chance of showing up at the top of the search results. That content originates via two steps:

1. Discover the questions people in your niche are asking.
2. Create content that answers their questions.

Most people use a search engine to find an answer to a question. If you can answer that question in your content, you gain a fan (and possibly a subscriber or customer for life). This was the unique advantage I had when I launched my first blog on career coaching. I had committed to answering all the career-related questions that accounting professionals had. The blog posts I published included these:

- How long should a resume be?
- Should I use a chronological or functional resume format?
- How do I get my foot in the door for a job interview?
- How should I handle a panel interview?
- What should I do if I went on a job interview but have heard nothing?

Now, when I first started out, I didn't know what the questions were. Maybe you feel that way too. On top of that, I didn't even know the answer to every career-related question every accounting professional might have. But I made it my business to find out. A great place to start is by using online tools that collect questions people are asking in the search engines. For an up-to-date list of my favorite tools, go to YourMessageMatters Book.com/tools.

You can also ask for people to submit questions on social media, find a forum where people go to ask questions, or even consider sending out a survey. Although I had a tiny mailing list of less than one hundred people my first year of blogging, I sent out a survey and asked them to share with me their biggest career-related questions. I used that first batch of responses to create my content over the next year.

If you take similar steps, over time your website will become a fantastic reservoir of answers. You'll have a body of work you can freely share with others. You'll create leverage with your advice and expertise. You'll help people, even on days when you're not working. Creating a strategy for coming up with content also permits you to charge what you are worth. You can know with assurance that you have something to offer everyone, whether they become a client or customer or not. Don't feel bad for people who cannot afford your paid advice. Simply direct them to all the free content you have created to help them.

### Free Traffic Source 2: Social Traffic

You've probably already noticed that social media can become a time thief if you're not careful. You can waste hours on end trying to be everywhere at once and in the end realize that for all that effort, you've reached no one.

For example, let's say you're at the beach, standing before the ocean holding a glass of water in one hand and a tiny vial of ink in the other. The ink in the vial represents the impact you can make with your time, energy, and effort, and the sources of water represent those who can hear your message.

Now let's say you have two choices. You can either pour the vial of ink into the ocean or pour it into the glass of water. Which action leads to the more significant impact on the water? The obvious answer is that you should pour the ink into the glass of water. Similarly, you are better off to pick one social media channel and go deep, pouring your time and energy into that one, rather than diluting your potential impact by spreading yourself too thin. On what social media platform is your audience hanging out the most? That is where you start.

Try this thirty-day experiment: Select one social media channel and decide to go all-in on learning that platform for thirty days. Intentionally ignore the other social platforms for now. Remember my brothers' and my search for the perfect fishing spot? You're on a search for a perfect fishing spot too. And sometimes you can make a fishing spot the perfect spot simply by the effort you put in. For now, I'd rather you put several poles in the water in one pond than put one pole in each of several ponds. We give ourselves the greatest chance for success when we focus on one thing at a time.

### Free Traffic Source 3: Subscriber Traffic

Subscriber traffic includes everyone on your mailing list. With just one tap of the Send button, you can direct thousands of people to any place you want online. Remember, this is traffic you control. You can instantly get eyes on your new blog post, podcast episode, or video. If your subscribers like the content, they may also share it on their own social media sites. This in turn will bring new people into your world.

These three categories are your best sources of free traffic, and free traffic is the ultimate traffic you want in your business. These three sources can yield great results, but you have to put the work in. The problem with most messengers is that they give up way too soon. They are not actively creating new, fresh content or building an email list. Remember our farming analogy? You want to become a farmer. Free traffic is like planting a garden in your backyard. You won't get results overnight. But once green beans grow in your garden, you can add them to your dinner menu any time you want.

But what should you do while you're waiting for your crop to grow? If I want green beans for dinner tonight and they aren't yet growing in my garden, what should I do? Go to the store and buy some. The same is true for your business. If you want to drive traffic to your site by the end of the day, then go to the traffic store and buy some.

## Paid Traffic: Cold, Lukewarm, Warm, and Hot

Paid traffic refers to the act of paying money to send targeted visitors to your site. It's traffic you can turn on and turn off at any time. If free traffic is like an old-fashioned water pump, then paid traffic is a water faucet. You've paid for the water; all you have to do is turn it on.

If you're frustrated with the lack of traffic you have to your site, you can buy some. The appeal of paid traffic is that you can get it instantly. Almost every social media site offers businesses, like yours and mine, the opportunity to place ads in front of our ideal audience. But we don't want to show our ads to just anyone. We only want to put our ads in front of the right people. We do that by choosing the right temperature.

Not all audiences are created equal. Not everyone in your niche is at the same point of awareness or understanding. That means you need to communicate differently to people at each stage of the journey. Think of every member of your audience as being in one of four temperature points: cold, lukewarm, warm, and hot.

Each traffic temperature has a single goal. In an ideal world, your potential customer will move from cold to hot. The goal of this section is to see paid traffic as a way of taking a customer on a journey through four levels of temperature.

### Cold Traffic: From Unaware to Aware

Cold traffic represents people who are your target audience but have no awareness of you or your brand. Your goal for cold traffic should be creating awareness. What's the best way to bring awareness to your business? A great place to start is to run paid ads that drive people to some of your most helpful content. Do you have any useful blog posts, podcasts, or videos to share? If not, you should soon. And once you do, you can advertise those to cold traffic. A cold traffic advertisement, which can also be called an "awareness campaign," begins the process of bringing targeted people into the top of your funnel. Often for just a few cents per click, you can introduce yourself to people who had no idea your website existed. Once they've consumed some of your free content, you can move them to the next step.

### Lukewarm Traffic: From Aware to Subscriber

People move to the lukewarm stage once they've become aware of you. At this point they have engaged with your content, but that's all they've done. The main objective for lukewarm traffic is to move them from awareness to becoming a subscriber.

Remember the Hourglass Funnel? Lukewarm traffic is at the top of the hourglass, but you've yet to capture them on your email list. Running ads to this audience is known as *retargeting*. Retargeting means they've visited your site, and now you are showing them an ad on social media encouraging them to come back. Here's an example of how retargeting works.

Let's say someone from your target audience saw a "cold" ad you ran on social media directing people to a blog post on your website. By clicking on the ad, they are sent to your blog post. We can assume they have some interest in your blog's topic or they wouldn't have clicked on the ad in the first place, right? Because they've visited your blog at some point in the past, you can show them yet another ad. The best type of ad to show lukewarm traffic is some type of download in exchange for their email address. Go back to chapter 13, about capturing leads, for some of my favorite ideas. All this work is designed to help you retarget people who are aware of you but are not on your email list.

### Warm Traffic: From Subscriber to Customer

Once someone becomes a subscriber, there is the potential for a relationship to develop. The stronger the relationship gets, the more likely they are to buy something from you.

Did you know if you have an email list, you can target those same people with ads on social media? Almost every social media ad platform has this capability. Start with the email list-building service you use and export your entire list into an Excel file. You then take that same Excel file and upload it to the social media ad platform of your choice. Once the system finds the matches, you'll have a list of warm leads to show ads to.

You may be wondering, *Why am I paying to show them an ad if they are already on my email list?* I had that same question too. The answer is simple actually. You'll never get 100 percent of your email list to open your emails. By showing ads to your list, you can let the maximum number of people know about your promotion. Remember, it's all about relevance. Don't waste money trying to sell to cold audiences. Only pitch to your warm and hot audiences. You need to have the right conversation at the right time.

### *Hot Traffic: From Customer to Repeat Buyer*

Hot traffic is your list of buyers. These are people who have purchased from you in the past. The goal with hot audience ads is to get them to buy from you again. Do you have a monthly membership site they may want to join? Do you have a coaching program they should enroll in? What do you have to offer as the next step for them? Customers who bought one of your products are the most likely to buy another. This is why having multiple income streams is so valuable. Not just because you have several products to sell, but because those sales help fuel each other.

## Your Paid Traffic Game Plan

You may be thinking, *Do I have to run ads to all four temperatures of my audience in order to be effective?* The decision of how deep you go with paid ads—that is, how many you buy and how much you spend—depends on where you are in your business journey. Most people don't realize you can get started for as little as five dollars per day. You don't have to have a large advertising budget in the beginning. As far as a strategy, you may want to start with luke-warm ads to build your list, or maybe you want to purchase warm ads to make some sales. You can build out your customer journey through paid traffic over time. To help you come up with the paid traffic plan that is right for you now, answer the following questions:

- Are you most in need of web traffic right now? Start with cold traffic ads.
- Do you want to build your email list faster? Run lukewarm traffic ads.
- Do you currently have a product you want to sell more of? Use warm ads to make more sales.

• Do you have more than one product or service? Consider running hot ads to your customers.

Obviously, you may not be at a place in your business yet where running all four types of ads at once makes sense. That's okay. The goal is not full-scale, immediate implementation of all your ad planning. Rather, the goal is the consistent promotion of your business and the movement of people in your audience from one stage in the journey to the next.

## Partner Traffic: Guest Contributor, Guest Teacher, and Guest Host

Who are some people who sell to your market but don't sell the type of product or service you offer? Answering this question will lead you to potential partners.

Just to recap, partners are other people in your niche who already have an established following. Partner traffic is the web traffic the partner sends to you from their email list. I'm sure you are wondering why they would do that. That's a great question. While there can be multiple reasons, the primary reason or motivation for a partner to send you traffic is something known as *affiliate income*.

Let's say you have an online course that sells for $500. As an incentive to your partner for sending you traffic, you agree to split the profit with them 50/50, meaning the partner makes $250 for every sale you make. The way we track this is through something known as an *affiliate link*. I don't want to get too technical here, just know there are easy-to-use software applications that can track this for you. You can view a list of some of my favorite ones at YourMessageMattersBook.com/tools.

This is just one example of how partner traffic can be a win for both parties. Gaining partner traffic is like being invited to a secret fishing hole on someone else's property. Like Joseph Nicoletti's story at the beginning of this chapter, partner traffic is a potential gold mine that can build your business quickly.

## Building Your Dream List of Partners

If you want to tap into the power of partner traffic, begin by building your dream list. Create a list of potential partners by asking, *Who's already having conversations with my target market?* Open a spreadsheet and begin to add names of influencers. Ask yourself the following questions:

- Which influencers have active blogs in my niche?
- Who is behind the popular podcasts in my niche?
- Who is running the most popular YouTube channels in my niche?
- Who has a popular following on (insert social media site) in my niche?

Keep adding names to your list until you've amassed one hundred potential partners. Or if you prefer, you can outsource this project and have someone else compile this list for you.

## Maximizing Results with Your Potential Partner List

Dan Sullivan of Strategic Coach teaches a process he calls the Top 20 Club and Farm Club.[2] From your list of one hundred, identify twenty potential partners who fit one of the following two statements:

- I believe I can partner with this person in the next ninety days.

- This person has an active audience but is not yet famous in my niche.

These top twenty names are where you should start. The rest of the names on your spreadsheet become your "farm club." You will focus 100 percent on reaching out and developing relationships with your top twenty. But just as in Major League Baseball, where each team has players in a minor league farm team who can be called up to play, once you get either a yes or a no, you will move a new name from your farm list into your top twenty. Focus on building relationships with those in your top twenty. Follow this simple strategy, and you'll have greater success than if you try to reach out to everyone.

Once you have your list, what do you do next? You have several options at your disposal. You don't have to take all three actions to be successful at building your business. In fact, I've used each of these at different times. There are no wrong moves, only opportunities for potential growth. The three partner traffic strategies can be categorized as guest contributor, guest teacher, or guest host. The questions below can help you decide which of these opportunities are best suited to you at any given time.

### Guest Contributor—Where can you join a conversation that's already happening online?

A great place to start building partner traffic is becoming a guest contributor. You don't need to have a large existing audience to be a contributor. You just need to have a message to share. There are three ways to become a guest contributor:

- *Guest posting*—Which websites online already serve your market and accept guest posts? If you enjoy writing, guest posting can be a great way to drive traffic back to your site. Did you know large media sites like *Forbes*, *Business Insider*, *Family Circle*, *Shape*, *Entrepreneur*, and *Self* are always on the hunt for guest writers? Here's the big secret: your favorite magazine, blog, or TV show runs on fresh content. It's what keeps the publication alive. Editors are always on the lookout for guest contributors who can make their job easier. Here's a simple way to get started. Go to a search engine and do one of the following searches: *topic* + "write for us" or *topic* + "submit a guest post." Replace the word "topic" with whatever main keyword fits your niche and you'll find plenty of opportunities to guest post.

- *Guest podcaster*—Which podcasts in your niche regularly interview guests? Just like editors are always on the lookout for guest writers, podcasters are always on the hunt for people to interview for their podcast. Most podcasters publish weekly episodes and prefer to have interviews lined up a month ahead of time in order to stay on schedule. Because of this, they are always looking to fill up their queue. Sometimes all it takes is to be a guest on one podcast and you'll have podcasters reaching out to you to be a guest on their show. Why is that? Because podcasters look through the episode listings of other podcasters to find new guests. After my first book was published in 2015, I had a streak of over thirty-two podcast interviews in a row without me having to request to be on their show. That's just how powerfully this strategy can work for you.

- *Guest video interviews*—Which influencers in your niche have been known to interview other experts via video? Don't forget about video interviews. I believe in the days ahead this style of interview will only get more popular. One common way this happens is over livestreaming. Many social media outlets support livestreaming, meaning users can go live on video with their phones or web cam. There are influencers who have a large following and like to bring in guests to interview. They go live to their audience and they bring you in as a guest to interview. This can bring additional exposure to your message and traffic to your site.

### Guest Teacher—Where can you add value to an audience by teaching?

Guest teaching is the strategy that Joseph Nicoletti went all-in with to build his business. He found a source of pain (people were struggling to learn Scrivener), created an online course to solve the problem, and sold it via partner webinars. This strategy accomplished three things all at once: it brought him traffic, leads, and sales. Guest teaching brings you traffic when your partner promotes your webinar to his existing list. It builds your list as people register for your webinar. It creates sales by promoting your course at the end of the live webinar. As mentioned before, the partner benefits because you share a percentage of all the sales made from the webinar. If you love to teach, you should consider employing the guest teacher strategy.

### Guest Host—What type of online event can you host that other influencers would be willing to promote?

This final partner traffic strategy has more moving parts and can take more time and effort to pull together, but the payoff can be much greater. As a guest host, you will host an online event that other influencers promote to their existing audience. The two most common online events are a partner virtual summit and a partner product launch.

A partner virtual summit is similar to a free online conference. As the host of a partner virtual summit, you will video interview fifteen experts or more in your niche. One of the best ways to find these experts to interview is to go to Amazon and find popular books on your subject. Authors almost never turn down an opportunity to be interviewed about the topic of their book. These interviews will be released the week of your virtual summit. Anyone with access to the internet can watch the interviews for free, but they must register with an email address in order to attend.

Do you see where this is going? As each person you interviewed promotes your virtual summit to their list, your email list will grow exponentially. The reason the people you interviewed want to promote your summit in the first place is twofold. First, they get free publicity because their interview will be shared to everyone who attends the summit. Second, they have the potential to earn income by getting a share of all of the sales from the summit. Hosting a virtual summit is the strategy that Cory Peppler of the parenting and tech advice blog Parenting Digital used to build his list from 153 to over 1,500 subscribers in a single week.

A partner product launch is even more complex than a partner virtual summit. But while it does require a lot of work, it's often worth it, as it's not unusual for the host to grow their email list by thousands in two weeks. There are four prerequisites you need to have in place for a partner product launch to work:

- an online course
- a marketing plan
- an affiliate tracking software
- affiliates to promote

The big picture goal is to open the doors for your core online course every six to twelve months and to invite new partners to promote each subsequent launch. Using this approach, you can introduce yourself to new potential audience members every time you pivot to a new list of partners. Each of your partners will send out to their list an email you've written and supplied to them. Their incentive to promote you is the opportunity to earn a commission from anyone on their list who buys your course.

You will need at least six to nine months to successfully plan and pull off a project like this. While it can be a lot of work, it's totally worth it. It's not uncommon to have fifty partners or more all promoting your website in a short span of two weeks. The greatest benefit to you is both the growth of your email list and the increase in your course sales.

## Your Ninety-Day Traffic Blueprint

We covered many traffic strategies in this chapter. It can be tempting to dabble a little bit into all of them. A far better approach is to selectively choose only one at a time and see it through to implementation. For this reason, I recommend the following four-step approach:

1. Choose just one traffic strategy at a time.
2. Run a ninety-day experiment.
3. Assess your results and identify the next strategy you want to try.
4. Repeat.

Those of us working to create a message-based business know that things are complicated enough without us making things harder. We make things harder when we dabble in multiple traffic strategies at once. For one thing, it divides our attention and resources. Secondly, shifting our resources around doesn't allow enough time for us to see if any one strategy will work. Force yourself to commit to the one strategy you've chosen for a minimum of ninety days. Keep it simple. Believe me, you'll reap the benefits.

# The Messenger Roadmap

## Connect—Which traffic source will you use?

You did it! We will now fill in the last section of the Messenger Road-map. In this chapter, you've learned several strategies for bringing web traffic to your site. In the long-term you'll want to implement several of these traffic strategies, but my goal for you now is to just choose one.

Question: Which traffic source will you use?

**Free Traffic**
- Search
- Social Media
- Subscriber

**Paid Traffic**
- Cold Traffic Ads
- Lukewarm Traffic Ads
- Warm Traffic Ads
- Hot Traffic Ads

**Partner Traffic**
- Guest Contributor
- Guest Teacher
- Guest Host

# PART 4

# LIVE YOUR MESSAGE

When I was just twenty-two, I was thrust into a speaking engagement with over six hundred church pastors in attendance. What made this challenge even scarier was that each audience member had a grading sheet in hand. Talk about pressure.

One of my required college classes was Homiletics, which is the art of crafting and delivering messages to an audience. Each year the class voted to determine the top three speakers in the class. Being nominated meant you received the opportunity to take part in a speaking competition attended by over six hundred pastors.

Some reward, right? I realize now that it's a fortunate problem for me to have had. But at the time, I was a scared college kid, and getting up in front of all those people with my knees knocking felt like a rather dubious blessing for all the work I'd put in.

I still remember some of the thoughts that raced through my mind:

- *Who am I to speak in front of all these pastors?*
- *Do I even have the ability to deliver a message that can impact others?*
- *What do I do if I stumble through my words or my mind goes blank?*

Right before I went onstage, as I sat in the front row waiting to speak, someone leaned over to me and said, "Do you know who's sitting behind you? It's the pastor of one of the largest churches in the southern United States. Just thought you should know."

Thanks, that just made it *much* easier.

I was scared out of my mind. Yet deep down in my soul was a desire to speak and influence others. At the same time, I had zero interest in being placed under the spotlight. I felt like an imposter. *There are already so many other speakers who are way better than I am*, I thought. How do I reconcile these two competing tensions in my heart?

Trying to look the part of an expert is exhausting. This is especially true when we compare ourselves to our competition. *Who are we to consider ourselves an expert*, we may ask, *when others are already executing at a high level?* In a recent survey to my email list, one respondent, Camille, summarized it best:

Why would someone listen to my message if I am a new voice on a well-covered subject? Can I be an "expert" if I have only personal anecdotes and don't have original research and/or data to back up what I'm saying? My message and platform feels like a folding table with a hand-lettered sign while my competition has a bigger booth with colorful awnings and a glittering array of inventory.

Getting noticed in our chosen field is hard work. To make things even more challenging, we have to compete with an already crowded marketplace. There's already so much noise being made. We become discouraged when the only solution we see is to shout louder than everyone else. If we can demand more attention, we can succeed (we tell ourselves). But placing a spotlight on ourselves was never our intended purpose.

It's hard to be an expert. But it's easy to be a guide. The goal of an expert is to prove to everyone they are the expert. The role of a guide is to simply serve others. Stop trying to be the hero, and start serving others as a guide.

As we will learn in the following chapters, a guide does three things well: encourages the heart, educates the head, and empowers the hands. Let's explore how to live that message of yours!

# 16

## Encouraging Hearts

*Moving People from Discouragement to Hope*

*The Lord of the Rings* and *The Hobbit* are some of the most beloved books ever written, but they almost didn't happen. Most of us can't imagine a world without Middle Earth, Bilbo Baggins, and Frodo's quest to destroy the ring. But if it wasn't for the encouragement of C. S. Lewis, J. R. R. Tolkien would never have written either classic.

In 1926, a year after Tolkien began teaching at Oxford University, he met C. S. Lewis at a faculty meeting. Four years later, they formed a small writing group known as *The Inklings*. The group met on Monday mornings to share poetry with one another. Eventually, the group expanded to nineteen individuals and covered all forms of writing. The meetings moved from Monday mornings to Thursday nights. Lewis was known to produce a pot of very strong tea as the men settled in and lit their pipes.

"Well, who has something to read to us?" Lewis would say to get things started. Someone always did. On they would go, late into the night, reading aloud their stories, offering advice, and encouraging one another. Tolkien would bring along a new chapter from *The Lord of the Rings*. Lewis would read aloud *The Screwtape Letters* to the group. If it wasn't for the encouragement of others, many classics never would have been completed.[1]

After Lewis's death in 1963, Tolkien wrote a heartwarming note to the Tolkien Society of America: "The unpayable debt that I owe to [Lewis] was not 'influence' as it is ordinarily understood but sheer encouragement. He was for long my only audience. Only from him did I ever get the idea that my 'stuff' could be more than a private hobby. But for his interest and unceasing eagerness for more I should never have brought [The Lord of the Rings] to a conclusion." Of the Inklings, Lewis said, "What I owe them all is incalculable. . . . Is any pleasure on earth as great as a circle of Christian friends by a good fire?"[2]

Encouragement grows in community. Discouragement grows in isolation. Whether you see it or not, discouragement lurks around every corner. Discouragement exists among the poor and the rich, the upper class and the middle class. Discouragement reaches across borders and touches every race and language. Discouragement abounds. But where discouragement brings darkness, hope brings the sunrise. Like the first warmth of sun on your skin, hope rejuvenates the soul.

People need hope before they need a solution. Hope offers power in the present moment. As John C. Maxwell says, "Where there is no hope in the future, there is no power in the present."[3] Before you sell, encourage the heart through hope. When you connect with the heart first, people will follow you anywhere. You don't build a following by laying out the best line of reasoning in an attempt to win people over. It just doesn't work that way.

Therapist Rabbi Edwin H. Friedman once pointed out, "The colossal misunderstanding of our time is the assumption that insight will work with people who are unmotivated to change.

Communication does not depend on syntax, or eloquence, or rhetoric, or articulation but on the emotional context in which the message is being heard."[4] Said another way, successful businessman and public servant Carl W. Buehner once pointed out, "They may forget what you said—but they will never forget how you made them feel."[5]

To be clear, connecting with the heart is not a sales strategy. It's not a manipulative move to get people to do what you want. To connect with the heart we must empathize with our audience's challenges. We must show we truly care. In order for the heart to open, you must be genuine. People can sense phoniness. But a leader with a genuine heart is a rare find.

While other influencers focus on being seen and heard, you will quietly go about your day sharing hope. Sharing hope through your writing. Sharing hope on your podcasts. Sharing hope on social media. Sharing hope on your videos. Choose to offer encouragement more than you offer a payment plan. When you connect with the heart, people will follow you anywhere.

## The Feel, Felt, Found Principle to Offering Hope

I first heard of the *feel, felt, found principle* at a sales training conference back in 2003. Although I learned about it in a sales-focused environment, I don't like to view it as a tool or strategy to be used to overcome sales objections. I see it as a principle to be used to gain people's trust and offer them hope.

The principle refers to something a person does long before they offer the sale. This is how the traditional method of the feel, felt, found principle is stated: *"I know how you feel. I've felt the same way, but here's what I've found."* Instead of a sales strategy, though, I see it as a formula for offering real hope. I like to phrase it this way:

*"You're not alone. I've failed too. But change is possible!"*

If we break down the above phrase into three parts, it looks like this:

1. "*You're not alone*"—offer community (feel).
2. "*I've failed too*"—admit failures (felt).
3. "*Change is possible*"—share successes (found).

By employing these three truths, you can better empathize with your audience and build a deeper connection. Let's take a closer look at how you can use these in a practical way.

### "You're Not Alone"—Offer Community

Discouragement thrives in isolation. Hope, on the other hand, thrives in community. Many people feel hopeless today because they think they're the misfit. They are the exception. They are the only one to struggle. In their eyes, everyone else has figured out how to move up, level up, make a change, and have success.

This is why social media often feels more exclusive than inclusive. As we do our endless scroll, we see other people's perfect lives, the "best of the best" posted each day on social media. The more we view the perfect lives of others, the more we isolate ourselves in feelings about our own shortcomings.

Real community does the opposite. It reaches out a hand and says, "It's okay. You're not alone." Too often people building a message-based business fill their social media feed with images that seem to display more success than they have. In an attempt to build an audience through their success and wealth, they end up pushing people further away. They distance themselves from the real struggles, challenges, and isolation their audience is facing. You don't want to make this mistake. Slow down the success train so people can jump on board. Start with where people are and they'll go on the journey with you.

When you truly believe offering hope is more important than selling a payment plan, your language will change as well. Your words will feel more inclusive than exclusive. Your words will focus on the audience, not on you. Your invitation to them is one of joining a mission, not of buying a product. Think of this in terms of

- we vs. I
- enroll vs. buy
- join vs. purchase
- mission vs. goal

Can you feel the difference? It feels more natural to invite someone to join a mission rather than buy a product. This is good news for those of you who hate selling. Spreading your message starts by helping people understand they are not alone.


### *"I've Failed Too"—Admit Failures*

Do you have any embarrassing photos from your childhood? I certainly do. One of them is a picture of me and my two brothers standing proudly in our superhero Underoos when we were kids. If you've never heard of Underoos, it's a brand of superhero underwear invented by entrepreneur Larry Weiss in 1977.[6] By the time the 1980s rolled around, Fruit of the Loom acquired them and Underoos became a raging hit.

Even better, the underwear came with a superhero T-shirt. My brothers and I proudly wore those superhero Underoos. We even tucked our T-shirts into our underwear to look more like our beloved superheroes. I was Superman and my two brothers were Batman and Spiderman. We loved pretending to be superheroes.

But what makes a superhero likable? Is it really their superpowers? Is it Spiderman's ability to scale the heights of Manhattan? Is it Ironman's supergenius intellect? Maybe it's Captain America's raw courage? Superheroes' powers are, indeed, impressive. But I believe that what makes superheroes likable is not their strength, but their vulnerability. We like Spiderman because he, like us, struggles with doubt and a bit of immaturity. We like Ironman because he too struggles with ego getting in the way. We like Captain America because his kindness causes him to be taken advantage of at times. Your failures, too, make you more relatable than your successes do.

What's great about this is that you don't have to put on a show. Being you is good enough. Sharing your past failures and struggles makes you more relatable. It offers hope to others that if you've made the journey so can they.

### "Change Is Possible"—Share Successes

While admitting failures plays a part in connecting with your audience, it's not the complete story. Our goal is not to form a support group, but to build a thriving business. We want to add value to people's lives whether they buy from us or not. But we do hope that some of them, even many of them, will become our clients or customers. And part of that involves showing them what they have to gain by listening to our messages.

As a messenger, you'll want to share stories of success, and the most powerful stories of success come from people you have helped. While it's okay to share your own story of change and success, you shouldn't be the center of attention. Remember, you're not the hero. You're just the guide.

## Life Is Best Lived on Mission in Community

In *The Hobbit*, the goal of Bilbo's external quest is quite obvious. Help the dwarves rid their homeland of the dragon and recapture their kingdom. But there's also an internal quest for Bilbo Baggins.

The internal quest was the call from isolation to community, from feeling hopeless to hopeful.

Bilbo is preoccupied with safety and comfort. He thinks being alone is his ultimate aim in life. In the opening chapter of *The Fellowship of the Ring*, the first book of the trilogy, we see Bilbo had "no close friends, until some of his younger cousins began to grow up." After Bilbo's farewell party, he exclaims, "I don't know half of you half as well as I should like; and I like less than half of you half as well as you deserve." He then vanishes without any goodbyes.

Bilbo mistakenly believed life was best lived in isolation. That's why later he would tell Gandalf that he wanted to find rest "in peace and quiet, without a lot of relatives prying around, and a string of confounded visitors hanging on the bell."

But the greatest lesson Bilbo discovers is that life is not best lived in isolation. The goal in life is not to arrive safely at death all alone. Life is best lived on mission in community. Bilbo Baggins comes to life when we hear him exclaim, "I'm going on an adventure!" We, too, can offer hope by inviting others to join us on a grand adventure.

# 17

## Educating Heads

### *Moving People from Doubt to Confidence*

"You're not fit to be a counselor." These were not the words Kary was expecting to hear from his professor. Ever since Kary was a teenage boy he had struggled with depression, thoughts of suicide, and even self-injury. He had been bullied as a child. He was made fun of for having a girl's name. To make matters worse he had a stuttering problem. But when it came to sharing his thoughts and the pain he was experiencing, he mostly kept it to himself.

Now this struggle had followed him into his college days and marriage. He was studying to be a counselor because he wanted to help others who were in pain. But his past was still following him. One night after he had just finished cutting himself again, he decided to tell the people closest to him the truth. The next day he went to his professor expecting to hear the words "Thanks for sharing," but instead he said, "You're not fit to be a counselor." Kary had hit rock bottom. Twenty-three years of frustrations and emotions hit him all at once.

One of the lowest points in Kary's life, however, ended up being the impetus for change. It didn't happen overnight, but Kary got the help he desperately needed. A few years later, once he had gone through the process of healing, he knew he needed to share his story. His story mattered. His message mattered. He wanted more than anything to bring purpose to people who doubted themselves, just as he once had.

That's when he began to write his story in a book. The book was entitled *Your Secret Name*.[1] It's a book about labels. According to Kary, we all place labels on our lives. We all believe the labels others give us. We journey through life living less than our best because we believe the lies the world tells us. The goal of his book is to help people shed the labels, stop pretending, and step into their true identity.

Today, Kary Oberbrunner is the founder of a company called Igniting Souls. He is the bestselling author of several books, and he has trained over 250,000 authors, speakers, and coaches.[2] What's the motivation behind his work? He wants to bring purpose to the doubting.

In the Messenger Manifesto we discussed in chapter 5, we find the phrase "bring purpose to the doubting." You'll be hard-pressed to find a niche or industry that isn't affected by the problem of doubt. As humans, we doubt. We doubt whether we are good enough. We doubt if we have what it takes. We doubt that we have a future. We doubt that we will overcome our current circumstances. We all doubt. As a guide, your role is to bring purpose to the doubting. How do you do that? By educating the head.

Why is this? Because doubt comes from a lack of understanding, and understanding begins with knowledge. If fear lives in the heart, doubt lives in the head. To help your audience overcome doubt, you must learn to "out-teach" the competition. How do you do this? You adopt the following three practices: (1) create content that delivers value, (2) distribute that content in multiple formats, and (3) cover a wide range of topics in a small niche. Let's take a look at how to do these three things.

## Deliver Valuable Content

Remember, your primary mission is to make a difference in people's lives. This is why creating free, valuable content for people to consume is so important. Do not tease people with your free content. Decide to hold nothing back. When you are generous with what you share, people will choose you over the competition because they are consistently learning from you. You must do more than just run people through a funnel that sells your products. That might gain you a sale, but it won't build you a following.

In fact, I'll go one step further and say give away your best stuff. The idea of freely giving away your best stuff scares many messengers. *If I give it all away for free, what will people buy from me?* But success is about more than just providing information. It's also about facilitating transformation. On top of the information we provide, we can offer support, community, accountability, and services. And that's something people are willing to pay for, especially once they've come to trust us.

People will also pay for convenience. Instead of reading a string of different blog posts, they will pay to get the content in a video course format. Or maybe they will prefer to get your content in the form of a hardcover book. The important thing to remember is this: Don't have a scarcity mindset with what you freely share. Just tell yourself, *There's more where that came from.* As we learned in a previous chapter, some of the primary ways we can add free value to people's lives are through blog posts, podcasts, and videos. By doing so, you'll create content that attracts your audience.

## Distribute Content into Multiple Formats

By this, I mean you want your content to be digestible in as many formats as possible. After you finish writing a blog post, consider ways to repurpose that content and use it in other ways. Develop podcasts that followers can listen to during their daily commute. Record videos for your audience to view on their phones. Host a webinar and teach your content in a live format. Use livestreaming to share your content on social media.

Members of your audience each have their own preferred style of learning. By repurposing your content, you'll be able to reach a wider audience. Some of my followers, for example, only listen to podcasts. Some of them only read blog posts. I can reach them all through repurposing. Here's a simple repurposing plan I use in my message-based business:

- *Organize your thoughts in a written blog post*—I prefer to start with writing because it helps me to disentangle my thoughts and get them into an organized outline. Once I'm finished writing and editing the post, I publish it.
- *Record a podcast episode using your written blog post as a script*—I then use my blog post as a script for my podcast. This isn't just an audio version of a blog post. I use the article as a speaker would use notes. I ad-lib on points I want to further explain. If I recall a relevant story, I share it. Once recorded, I schedule the podcast.
- *Convert the blog post into a video*—You can also use your written text to record a video. If you write blog posts using the format I shared in the previous section, you'll be able to easily convert your post into a video. Each blog post I write has three to five subpoints. This approach easily translates into an outline for future video recording.

- *Create snippets of each format to share on social media—*
  Whether you do it yourself or delegate this task to a team-
  mate, you'll want to create short snippets of your content
  and post them on social media sites to get the attention
  of people who can benefit from your business. You can lift
  quotes from your blog posts, or grab audio sound bites
  from your podcast or video snippets of your videos and
  use them to tease out your content to all the major social
  media sites.

## Cover a Wide Range of Topics

The best way to cast a wide net is to decide to answer every question in your niche. Cover it all. Don't just cover the topics you
enjoy the most. If needed, do some extra learning on the side so
you have more to offer. Seek out information about questions to
which you don't already know the answer. Research and write
about any topic that falls under your umbrella niche.

When I first launched my career blog for accountants, I had a
tendency to only cover topics regarding resumes. It was a topic
I felt the most comfortable addressing. But my audience wasn't
only searching for resume help. They were seeking information
and answers on accounting career options, job interviews, salary
negotiations, and how to recover from being fired.

By setting the intention to answer every question in your niche,
you'll become more well rounded while casting a wider net to
attract your audience. Use the tips we shared in chapter 12 on
content creation to help you easily find and create content your
audience will love.

Following this three-step content approach will help you out-
teach the competition. Through repurposing a single idea to multiple content formats, you'll be working smarter, not harder. The

goal of all of this content sharing is to build trust with your audience. But at the end of the day, we don't want them just to consume our information. We want them to do something. Next, I'll share with you the three best ways to move your audience from delay to action.

# 18

## Empowering Hands

### *Moving People from Delay to Action*

I was sitting in a hotel conference room in Dallas, Texas, on the second day of a private mastermind meetup. I was in the room with a dozen close friends when one individual piped up and said, "Before we go, let's take turns putting each person in a 'hot seat' and share with them what we think their superpower might be."

Since we knew each other well, this seemed like a great idea. Most people discount their own gifts or underestimate the value they bring. Why not end our time together being reminded of how each of us shows up best? The room was electrifying as words like *charismatic*, *motivational*, *insightful*, and *thought-leader* were thrown out to describe various participants. Then, it was my turn.

I squirmed in the seat, a bit curious what my peers would say. That's when someone shouted out, "You're Mr. Practical." The room unanimously and enthusiastically agreed. It all happened so fast. *Wait*, I thought, *I was hoping to go around the room and hear several thoughts and ideas. Maybe even a better word than* practical.

I must admit, I left the conference room a bit discouraged that day. My superpower is "Mr. Practical"? At the time, I thought *practical* equaled *boring*. But the more I looked over my body of work in the following days, the more I realized they were right. My books, courses, blog posts, podcasts, and videos were all indeed very practical.

Over the next few weeks, I began to see just how powerful "practical" could be. That's when I bumped up against the truth we've already touched on several times: those of us looking to build a business don't suffer from a lack of options, we suffer from having too many. Given that reality, one of the best gifts you can give when sharing your message is practical simplicity.

One of your main roles as a guide is to offer direction to the confused. The people you most want to help are simply overwhelmed. They are overwhelmed with options, information, and advice. They are listening to too many voices. Their email inbox is flooded with options and choices. But what our audience needs to hear from us is that success isn't that complicated.

The people you want to serve feel confused by too many choices. Our goal as the guide is to point the way forward for them. When it comes to offering direction to the confused, the following three tried-and-true principles work in any market: give the gift of clarity, design a teaching tool, and deliver quick wins.

## Give the Gift of Clarity

German-British statistician and economist E. F. Schumacher, in his essay "Small Is Beautiful," wrote, "Any intelligent fool can make things bigger, more complex. . . . It takes a touch of genius—and a lot of courage to move in the opposite direction."[1] Your role as a guide is to bring simplicity to the complexity your audience faces. They simply do not yet see what you see. It's like the saying

"It's hard to read the label when you're inside the bottle." Maybe you've been in the bottle yourself. But you see something now that your audience does not, and you can offer them a simpler way.

The challenge for many guides is that they face the curse of knowledge. The curse of knowledge occurs when we forget what it's like to be a beginner. A brilliant professor may forget what it's like to be a freshman student. A subject matter expert may forget what it's like to be a novice on the topic. The curse of knowledge presents a challenge for us in two unique ways.

### Challenge 1: Undervaluing the Basics

Once we advance in our understanding of a particular subject, we tend to overlook the tremendous value of the basics. The basics strike us as being understood, implied, or common knowledge. We fail to realize that many beginners with zero knowledge and understanding are discovering our topic for the first time. In Eugene Schwartz's classic book, *Breakthrough Advertising*,[2] he breaks down the customer journey into five distinct phases:

1. *The Most Aware*: Your prospect knows you, trusts you, and knows your product. The only step left is the buying decision.
2. *Product-Aware*: Your prospect knows they need a solution and discovers you have a product that can help.
3. *Solution-Aware*: Your prospect becomes aware of the solution to their problem but doesn't know you have a product.
4. *Problem-Aware*: Your prospect becomes aware of their problem but is not sure what to do about it.
5. *Completely Unaware*: Your prospect is not even aware that they have a problem.

With each step further down this list, the size of your audience grows larger. This is why the value of teaching the basics can be so powerful. It brings value to the largest segment of your audience by making them more competent in the area in which you have more to offer them. Don't diminish the tremendous value of teaching the basics.

### Challenge 2: Sharing Conceptual Thoughts Over Concrete Actions

Since we're more familiar with our own subject matter, we tend to be more stimulated by advanced theory and conceptual thinking. Concrete steps seem understood or obvious to us. But most of our audience just wants clarity on the next step. Clarity is more valuable to them than conceptual thought.

This is especially true for those in the problem-aware stage. When someone becomes aware of a problem, their natural next step is to seek out a solution. Off they go, seeking answers via articles, podcasts, and videos. This is why as a guide, you should be comprehensively and systematically answering all the basic questions you can think of in your niche via blog posts, podcasts, and videos. It's the fastest way to bring people into your world. You have the solution and the products for their biggest challenges.

Giving the gift of clarity is as simple as answering the most common questions in the most practical ways. This simple strategy has allowed me to build two unique online businesses from scratch. Overlook the basics to your peril. Fight against the curse of knowledge and give the gift of clarity to your audience.

## Design a Teaching Tool

Can you clearly articulate in a few steps how your ideal audience can become successful? Can you put on a single piece of paper your process for taking your ideal customers from where they are now to where they want to be? Whether you're a business coach, speaker, trainer, writer, or consultant, you need a clearly defined process, unique to you, that walks your audience through the steps to success. So my question is this: Do you have the steps clearly laid out?

Before I start writing a book, I always design a big-picture teaching tool. Examples of two such teaching tools included in this book are the Hourglass Funnel and the Messenger Roadmap. A good book should take the reader on a journey. Reading it should be a transformational process. The goal of the book is to help your ideal reader think differently and act differently than they did before. Creating a visual teaching tool of your success path forces you as a teacher, speaker, or coach to stop talking circles around concepts and start getting specific and practical. Remember, your audience isn't seeking information, but transformation.

As the guide, you should be asking this question: How can I break my message down into step 1, step 2, step 3, etc.? This is a question I ask myself when I start a new book project. Once I lay out a teaching tool for my audience, my ideal clients can easily self-identify where they are on the map. This gives them clarity on what their next best step should be and shows them how I, as the guide, can help. This allows me to create a "brand" instead of just offering a "talk." The success path is the very center of my message. It's the hub of all the other income streams. This teaching tool becomes

- the chapter outline of my book
- the topics of my keynote talks
- the parts of my membership site or online course
- the main subject of my event, workshop, or retreat
- a coaching tool I use with clients
- and much more.

Creating a teaching tool is one of the most strategic steps you can take. Still not convinced? Here are three powerful reasons you need a teaching tool:

### Reason 1: A teaching tool helps your audience gain a visual understanding.

Having a teaching tool that your audience can visually see helps the lightbulb switch on in their minds. That's because the steps allow them to see a visual path of transformation. Some of my favorite books of all time use the concept of including a visual teaching tool. These include

- Stephen Covey's 7 *Habits of Highly Effective People*
- Jim Collins's Hedgehog Concept in his book *Good to Great*
- Donald Miller's StoryBrand framework

Designing a teaching tool can help connect customers to your process in a powerful way. Creating a visual teaching tool serves as a map. It gives your customers hope that there is a plan and tells them that you are the guide who can help them. If you'd like to view and download a visual roadmap of this book, go to YourMessageMattersBook.com/tools.

### Reason 2: A teaching tool gives your audience a pathway of belonging.

When you provide a visual success path, you build trust with your audience. It gives them a sense of belonging that you know what you're doing and you, as the guide, have a plan for them. Your customers can see a long-term development plan, which breeds trust and longevity. It's much easier for them to say yes to going on a journey with you. No one wants to waste time. If your plan makes it easy for me, the customer, to see both the forest and the trees, I'm much more likely to let you be the guide. I have more confidence to enter the woods if I have both a guide and a map. You are the guide. Your teaching tool is the guide's map.

### Reason 3: A teaching tool forces you to get clarity on your own message.

The process of designing your own success path will drive you to pursue simplicity. It will force you to break down all the complex parts into simple steps. Our job as a speaker, coach, blogger, or consultant is to wrestle with complex subjects until we can break them down to their simplest parts. Our job as the guide is to wrestle with our topic until we can clearly articulate it in a simple plan.

Once you have your teaching tool designed, two amazing opportunities will open up for you. First, you can see all the different ways you can communicate with your teaching tool. You will recognize individual keynote talks you can give and coaching programs you can launch, how a membership site model can work, and much more.

Second, you can begin to create multiple income streams one product at a time. For me, it made the most sense to turn the different elements of my teaching tool into the chapters of a book. Once my first book was launched, I redesigned my membership site to fit my success path. From there, I launched a coaching program to help people progress through the success path. As I mentioned previously, this is the plan I followed until I had created seven income streams in under twelve months. There's power in creating multiple income streams from one core message.

## Deliver Quick Wins

Give someone a "quick win" and you'll have a fan for life. What's a single transformative step that's so easy to take it's impossible for your audience to fail at it? Delivering a quick win doesn't have to be complicated. A quick win can be delivered as a

- simple tool
- one-page cheat sheet
- checklist
- resource list
- useful worksheet
- helpful spreadsheet
- action guide
- mind map
- blueprint

Most of these can be created in under thirty minutes. Give someone a quick win, and they will want more from you. Don't underestimate the power of simplicity. Most of the influencers I follow today are people whose importance to me can be traced back to a quick win they gave me. They empowered me to take action. You can empower your audience to take action by giving them the gift of clarity, by designing a success path, and by delivering quick wins.

## It's Time to Live Your Message

You now have the tools to successfully live your message daily. As you show up each day to serve your audience, choose to move them forward in the following three ways:

- encouraging hearts: moving people from discouragement to hope
- educating heads: moving people from doubt to confidence
- empowering hands: moving people from delay to action

Just as Rome wasn't built in a day, neither will your business. What does build your business is consistently showing up every day and serving your people well. But before we release you to go on your mission, there are three important mindsets you'll need to carry with you.

# 19

# The Messenger's Game Plan for Success

It was the second day of a live event I was hosting in Jacksonville, Florida. The afternoon break was winding down when an attendee caught my attention and handed me a plain manila folder. The tab of the folder read "1972 Miami Dolphins." I had no clue where this conversation was going. After all, the event was about marketing and how to build a business online, not about the history of American football.

I opened the folder to discover a single sheet of paper with words typed in an old-fashioned typewriter font.

"What is this?" I asked.

"It's the official playbook of the 1972 Miami Dolphins," he told me.

At first, I thought, *No way that can be true. It's a single sheet of paper. Don't most NFL teams have a large binder of complicated plays with x's and o's?* But I took a closer look and asked more questions.

It turned out that this sheet of paper was in fact the one-page summary of the defensive playbook of the 1972 Miami Dolphins. Most of the page was written in football lingo that any fan would enjoy, but one sentence in particular stood out to me. It read, "If we are going to accomplish our goals this year, it will require three things of us: (1) an INTENSE DESIRE; (2) a DESIRE TO IMPROVE; and (3) a WILLINGNESS TO WORK."

*Wow*, I thought. Because in that moment a realization hit me: All three of these keys are things that are accomplished behind the scenes. Things that are practiced away from the crowds and the lights on Sunday. These are Monday through Saturday mindsets. Mindsets that lead to particular habits and behaviors.

Most of us mistakenly think professional athletes have it easy. After all, they have big homes and large bank accounts. For the most part, they've already accomplished their goal of making it to the NFL, right? Hasn't their intense desire for something already been fulfilled? They are obviously talented to have made it to the top of their game, so a need to improve can't be a big motivator, correct? With all of the money, fortune, fame, and lavish lifestyles that the NFL can bring, is a willingness to work something these guys even put much thought into?

Then, the unexpected happened.

"Take a look at this." The conference attendee placed a ring in my hand.

I looked at it closely. It was the Super Bowl ring of the undefeated Miami Dolphins from 1972.

"How do you have this?" I asked.

"My dad was the defensive coordinator of the 1972 Dolphins" was his reply.

I couldn't believe I was actually holding a Super Bowl ring. Since I was a kid, I've watched the Super Bowl every year on television. Then, it dawned on me. Here in my hand was evidence of what can happen when someone makes a plan and sticks to it. By focusing on and valuing just three core mindsets, the 1972 Miami Dolphins were able to become Super Bowl champions. The truth is that these three mindsets can work for us too.

## 1. It Begins with an Intense Desire

When it comes to making your mark on the world, do you have an intense desire? Do you trust that your message matters? Do you believe that your story, experience, message, or passion can make a difference in the lives of others? Only you can move your message forward. It starts with you and it begins with an intense desire.

## 2. A Desire to Improve

Most of us want to see fast results, not incremental improvement. One of my favorite basketball coaches of all time is John Wooden. He did more than teach players the game of basketball. He taught men how to be successful in life. One of my favorite quotes of his speaks to both the desire to improve and the value of focusing on the little things: "When you improve a little each day, eventually big things occur. When you improve conditioning a little each day, eventually you have a big improvement in conditioning. Not tomorrow, not the next day, but eventually a big gain is made. Don't look for the big, quick improvement. Seek the small improvement one day at a time. That's the only way it happens—and when it happens, it lasts."[1]

If you want to excel in business, you must major in the little things that lead to success. Most entrepreneurs overlook the power of little things. A desire to improve is not about commitment to the big things. The secret of success is about doing a lot of little things well. Match your desire to improve with an intense focus on the little things.

## 3. A Willingness to Work

People tend to fall in love with the idea of a thing, but not love the work it takes to make the thing happen. Most people fall in love with the idea of writing a book, but not the work it takes to bring a book into the world. Most people fall in love with the idea of making a difference in the world, but not the work it takes to bring that message to the world. But you can do this differently. Choose to fall in love with the work. Show up each day and bring joy to your tasks and projects.

I often coach others to adopt the brick-by-brick philosophy. Every major action you take in your business lays another brick in the foundation of your business. You won't build a wall in a day, but over time your wall will get built. Every blog post you publish, every podcast you record, every video you upload, and every webinar you host lays another brick into a beautiful business you are building.

After carefully holding the Super Bowl ring in my hand on the day of my live event (and after showing the ring off to a few other people), I gave it back.

"Wait, there's more to this story," the ring's owner said.

He went on to tell me that the Miami Dolphins had made it to the Super Bowl the year before their big win, but they were embarrassed by the Dallas Cowboys, 24–3. In the locker room after the loss, Don Shula, their future Hall of Fame Coach, addressed the team. "I want you to remember how you feel in this moment. I know it's painful, but embrace it. Embrace the anger, frustration, sadness, and disappointment." He paused for a few moments, then said, "Now, I want you to determine to never feel this way again."

The very next year, the Miami Dolphins would go on to win the ring I'd just held in my hand.

## Your Mission, Should You Choose to Accept It

On completion of this book, you now know the roadmap to building a business with your message. A business that offers you more freedom, while making a difference in the lives of others. I can't wait to see what you do with it. But before I let you go, allow me to leave you with six practical steps to follow. Think of these as the messenger's game plan for success.

1. *Believe your message matters.* People are waiting for your help. They are waiting just on the other side of your present courage. Every person's story you've read in the pages of this book began with a moment of present courage. If you don't write your message, say it, or record it, it may never be heard by those who need to hear it.

2. *Define your message to ignite your message.* Getting clear about your message comes down to three things: purpose, people, and passion. You don't *find* your purpose, you *uncover* your purpose. It's already buried deep inside you. Next, find the people you most want to serve, and serve them well. You find your passion when you find a problem to solve. Serve others by helping them solve their greatest challenges.

3. *Become the guide, not the hero.* Instead of trying to become a celebrity, choose instead to serve others. Build an audience by creating a powerful message that encourages the heart, educates the head, and empowers the individual.

4. *Market your message using the four keystone habits—create, capture, compile, and connect.* Maintain your focus by organizing your week in the only four areas that matter to a messenger. Create content that builds trust with your audience. Capture your followers on an email list where you can build a relationship with them. Compile your knowledge into products and services. Connect with your audience where they are already hanging out.

5. *Fill out the Messenger Roadmap in the back of this book.*
Flip over a few more pages and you'll find a one-page map you can fill out to help you remember and implement the strategies in this book. This roadmap can serve as a guide to help you take action on everything you've learned.

6. *Take the Thirty-Day Messenger Manifesto Challenge.* To increase your focus and productivity, read the Messenger Manifesto—mine, or the one you custom created—out loud each morning for thirty days. Watch your confidence soar, your focus improve, your productivity multiply, and your business grow.

As I begin my day, I will choose to work from a place of mission and not fear, service and not greed, humility and not pride. I choose today to offer hope to the discouraged, purpose to the doubting, and direction to the confused. May this be my vision as I work today to build the business.

Do this and you'll make your mark on the world. Oh, and one more thing. Never forget . . .

*Your message matters.*

# Acknowledgments

I forgot how hard it is to write a book. While the writing process is never easy, it's absolutely worth it. To write a good book, it requires a village. Behind every author is a team of immensely talented individuals silently going about their daily work. Each day they offer their gifts to bring other people's messages to the world. While these "message carriers" may go unnoticed by the average reader, they are champions to authors like me.

It starts with a supportive family. As I mentioned in the dedication, this book never would have seen the light of day without the constant support and encouragement from my wife of twenty-two years, Charity. You were the one voice in my ear early on that told me I'd write and publish a book one day. I love you with all my heart. A big thank-you to my kids, Kayla and Jordan. My prayer is as you grow older, the words of this book will be a guiding light for you. Your message matters, and the world needs your gift to shine bright!

To my parents, thank you for being a godly example to me all these many years. Dad, I'm grateful to you as a coach, mentor, parent, and friend. Growing up as the son of a basketball coach has taught me many life lessons. Several of these lessons made their way into the pages of this book. Mom, thank you for your spirit of optimism and a never-ending thirst for learning. You instilled in me early to set goals and go after my dreams. To the rest of my family, I'm grateful for your support. Thank you, Joel, Jason, Kristi, Erin, Kyan, Kyle, and Kinley. A special thanks to my in-laws, Cliff and Opal Player, and the rest of the Player family (there are just way too many of you to name here).

I am grateful to Chad Allen, my literary agent. I still remember the day you challenged me to get a book proposal together. I naively thought I could put one together over the weekend. Your patience, persistence, and guidance breathed life into what became *Your Message Matters*. I'm deeply grateful for your creative input, constructive feedback, and countless hours of insights.

A huge thanks to Rachel Jacobson from Baker Books. Rachel, this book never would have happened without your early enthusiasm for what it could be. I couldn't have asked for a better partner. You led the project with impressive efficiency, leadership, patience, and encouragement. Thank you to the excellent team at Baker Books, including Patti Brinks, Melanie Burkhardt, Eileen Hanson, Olivia Peitsch, Janelle Wiesen, and Abby Van Wormer.

To Shari MacDonald Strong, I'll be forever grateful that you were my developmental editor. You use the right balance of positivity—pushing me to be better, calling out what needed to be improved—along with patience and encouragement to complete the task. You breathed life into this book. Thank you!

To my mentors, I am eternally grateful for your books, online courses, workshops, personal mentoring, and coaching. These include Michael Hyatt, Dan Miller, Ryan Levesque, Ryan Deiss, and Russell Brunson.

I want to thank all of my entrepreneur friends who allowed me to share their stories in this book. That list of influencers includes Chandler Bolt, Jeff Brown, Kimanzi Constable, Bob Lotich, Joseph Nicoletti, Kary Oberbrunner, Crystal Paine, Cory Peppler, Luria Petrucci, and Natalie Sisson.

To Roxanne Oates, my online business manager, thank you. Writing the manuscript pulled me away for several months from the day-to-day operations of the business. You flawlessly stepped in and ran the organization without skipping a beat. This book would have taken twice as long to write without your skills and dedication. Thank you.

Special thanks are also in order to the rest of our internal team, including Bryan Buckley, Jodie Von Kamecke, Val Brown, Timothy Link, Amy Stark, Realyn Sarzuelo, Cory Peppler, Antonette Cheng, Jennifer Gella, Varinder Pal, and Susan Elizabeth. Your daily contribution and dedication to our company's vision do not go unnoticed. Thank you for all you do to help other messengers get their stories heard.

# Appendix

## The Messenger Roadmap

| Your Acronym | Your Message Defined |
|---|---|
| | I help _____ (people)<br>to _____ (passion)<br>by _____ (purpose). |

| The Messenger Manifesto |
|---|
| *As I begin my day, I will . . .* |

| The Messenger Focusing Habits | |
|---|---|
| **Connect**<br>Which traffic source will you use? | |
| **Create**<br>What content type will you use to attract your audience? | |
| **Capture**<br>What tools will you use to capture leads? | |
| **Compile**<br>What will you sell to help your audience? | |

# Notes

### Introduction

1. Russell Conwell, *Acres of Diamonds* (New York: Harper & Brothers, 1915).
2. John C. Maxwell, *The 15 Invaluable Laws of Growth* (New York: Center Street, 2012), 25.
3. Russell Brunson, *Dotcom Secrets* (New York: Morgan James Publishing, 2015), 5–6.
4. "Top 10 Singers Who Get Famous through YouTube," BecomeSingers.com, June 10, 2018, https://www.becomesingers.com/singing-career/singers-who-get -famous-through-youtube.

### Part 1 Believe Your Message

1. Suzy Kassem, "Quotes," accessed May 8, 2020, suzykassem.com.
2. Dan Sullivan, "How to Build Your Own Confidence at Will," Strategic Coach, https://resources.strategiccoach.com/business-growth-and-strategy/how -to-build-your-own-confidence-at-will.

### Chapter 1 What Exactly Is a Messenger?

1. Bruce Wilkinson, Heather Kopp, and David Kopp, *The Dream Giver* (Colorado Springs: Multnomah, 2003), 12.
2. Wilkinson, Kopp, and Kopp, *Dream Giver*, 14–15.
3. Brendon Burchard, *The Motivation Manifesto* (Carlsbad, CA: Hay House, 2014), 3.
4. Wilkinson, Kopp, and Kopp, *Dream Giver*, 29.

259

## Chapter 2 Why Your Message Matters

1. Raymond R. Anderson, "The Natural History of Pikes Peak State Park," Iowa Department of Natural Resources, November 4, 2000, https://s-iihr34.iihr .uiowa.edu/publications/uploads/GSI-070.pdf.

2. "Leo Buscaglia Quotes," BrainyQuote, accessed November 17, 2019, https:// www.brainyquote.com/quotes/leo_buscaglia_150305.

3. "Andrew Clemens Created Art from Grains of Sand," Live Auctioneers, accessed May 2, 2019, https://www.liveauctioneers.com/news/be-smart/andrew -clemens-created-art-from-grains-of-sand.

4. Neal Gabler, *Walt Disney* (New York: Vintage Books, 2007), 137–38.

5. Gabler, *Walt Disney*, 137–38.

6. "John Wayne Quotes," accessed May 3, 2020, https://www.quotes.net/quote /64069.

7. Martin Luther King Jr., "Living Under the Tensions of Modern Life," *The Papers of Martin Luther King, Jr.*, vol. 6, ed. Claiborne Carson and Susan Carson (Berkeley: University of California Press, 2007), 265.

8. Sharon L. Lechter and Robert T. Kiyosaki, *Rich Dad's Prophecy* (New York: Grand Central Publishing, 2002), 208.

9. Steven Pressfield, *Turning Pro* (New York: Black Irish Entertainment, 2012), 72.

10. Zig Ziglar, *Raising Positive Kids in a Negative World* (Nashville: Thomas Nelson, 2002), 220.

11. "Andrew Clemens Created Art from Grains of Sand."

## Chapter 3 The Secret to Building a Business and Life You Love

1. Zig Ziglar, *Over the Top* (New York: HarperCollins Leadership, 1997), 12.

2. Ladan Nikravan Hayes, "Living Paycheck to Paycheck Is a Way of Life for Majority of U.S. Workers, According to New CareerBuilder Survey," Career-Builder, August 24, 2017, http://press.careerbuilder.com/2017-08-24-Living-Pay check-to-Paycheck-is-a-Way-of-Life-for-Majority-of-U-S-Workers-According -to-New-CareerBuilder-Survey.

3. Amy Adkins, "Employee Engagement in U.S. Stagnant in 2015," Gallup, January 13, 2016, https://news.gallup.com/poll/188144/employee-engagement-stag nant-2015.aspx.

4. "5 Whys: Getting to the Root of a Problem Quickly," Mind Tools, https:// www.mindtools.com/pages/article/newTMC_5W.htm.

## Chapter 4 Why You Should Build a Business Sharing Your Advice

1. Chandler Bolt, "About Self-Publishing School," Self-Publishing School, https://self-publishingschool.com/about-sps.

2. Gilbert King, "Charles Proteus Steinmetz, the Wizard of Schenectady," *Smithsonian Magazine*, August 16, 2011, https://www.smithsonianmag.com /history/charles-proteus-steinmetz-the-wizard-of-schenectady-51912022.

3. Dan Miller, *48 Days to the Work You Love* (Nashville: B & H, 2007), 181.

4. Jonathan Acuff, *Start* (Brentwood, TN: Lampo Press, 2013), 172.

## Chapter 5  The Messenger Manifesto

1. Michael Hyatt, *Your Best Year Ever* (Grand Rapids: Baker Books, 2018), 160.
2. Natalie Sisson, "About Me," https://www.nataliesisson.com/about.
3. Bronnie Ware, *The Top Five Regrets of the Dying* (Carlsbad, CA: Hay House, 2012).
4. Michael D'Antonio, *Hershey* (New York: Simon & Schuster, 2007).
5. David Novak, *Law and Theology in Judaism* (Brooklyn: KTAV Publishing House, 1976), 125.
6. Theodore Roosevelt, quoted in John C. Maxwell, *Everyone Communicates, Few Connect* (New York: HarperCollins Leadership, 2010), 187.
7. *Dead Poets Society*, directed by Peter Weir (Burbank, CA: Touchstone Pictures, 1989).
8. *The Karate Kid*, directed by John G. Avildsen (Los Angeles: Delphi II Productions, 1984).
9. Kristen Brennan, "Joseph Campbell," MoonGadget, 2006, http://www.moongadget.com/origins/myth.html.
10. *Star Wars Episode V: The Empire Strikes Back*, directed by Irvin Kershner (Universal City, CA: Lucasfilm, 1980).

## Chapter 6  The Ignite Your Message Framework

1. TVSA Team, "Hein Makes Survivor History," TVSA, September 6, 2007, https://www.tvsa.co.za/user/blogs/viewblogpost.aspx?blogpostid=12722.
2. Max Alexander, "Geothermal Heat Pump: How It Works," This Old House, 2017, https://www.thisoldhouse.com/ideas/geothermal-heat-pump-how-it-works.
3. Michael Hyatt, *Free to Focus* (Grand Rapids: Baker Publishing Group, 2019), 18–19.
4. Benjamin Hardy, *Willpower Doesn't Work* (New York: Hachette Books, 2018), 85.

## Chapter 7  Purpose: What Is Your Unique Gift?

1. Steven Rich, "How the Spindletop Oil Discovery Changed Texas and U.S. History," Drillers.com, July 1, 2018, https://drillers.com/spindletop-oil-discovery/.
2. Brian Dixon, *Start with Your People* (Grand Rapids: Zondervan, 2019), 142.
3. Jayson DeMers, "Do You Have Shiny Object Syndrome? What It Is and How to Beat It," *Entrepreneur*, February 9, 2017, https://www.entrepreneur.com/article/288370.
4. Alana Semuels, "The Authors Who Love Amazon," *The Atlantic*, July 20, 2018, https://www.theatlantic.com/technology/archive/2018/07/amazon-kindle-unlimited-self-publishing/565664.
5. T. J. McCue, "E Learning Climbing to $325 Billion by 2025," *Forbes*, July 31, 2018, https://www.forbes.com/sites/tjmccue/2018/07/31/e-learning-climbing-to-325-billion-by-2025-uf-canvas-absorb-schoology-moodle/#2b4c82173b39.

6. Pete Vargas III, "About Me," Advance Your Reach, https://advanceyour reach.com/about.

7. John LaRosa, "U.S. Personal Coaching Industry Tops $1 Billion, and Growing," Market Research, February 12, 2018, https://blog.marketresearch.com/us -personal-coaching-industry-tops-1-billion-and-growing.

8. Timothy D. Wilson, *Redirect* (New York: Back Bay Books, 2011), 62–63.

## Chapter 8 People: Who Do You Want to Help?

1. Crystal Paine, "About Me," Money Saving Mom, https://moneysavingmom .com/about.

2. Brendon Burchard, *The Millionaire Messenger* (New York: Free Press, 2011), 48.

## Chapter 9 Passion: What Problem Will You Solve?

1. Kimanzi Constable, "About Me," https://kconstable.com/about.

2. Erin Hawkins, "Rogers Reflects on 'Castaways' Experience," *Sequim Gazette*, October 3, 2018, https://www.sequimgazette.com/news/rogers-reflects-on -castaways-experience/.

## Chapter 10 Mission Control: Establishing Your Home Base

1. Roy Rosenzweig and Elizabeth Blackmar, *The Park and the People* (Ithaca, NY: Cornell University Press, 1992), 513.

## Chapter 11 Extraordinary Focus Leads to Success

1. "U.S. Slackline Walker Dean Potter Crosses China Canyon," BBC News (Asia), April 23, 2012, https://www.bbc.com/news/av/world-asia-17811115/us -slackline-walker-dean-potter-crosses-china-canyon.

## Chapter 12 Create: Get Your Message Out to the Masses

1. "The Pickwick Papers," Charles Dickens Info, https://www.charlesdickens info.com/novels/pickwick-papers.

2. Jeff Goins, *Real Artists Don't Starve* (New York: HarperCollins Leadership, 2017), 125.

3. Bob Lotich, "About Me," SeedTime, https://seedtime.com/about.

4. Jeff Brown, "About Me," Read to Lead podcast, https://readtoleadpodcast .com/about.

5. Luria Petrucci, "About Me," Live Streaming Pros, accessed July 15, 2019, https://livestreamingpros.com/luria.

6. Paul Smith, *Lead with a Story* (New York: American Management Association, 2012), 11.

7. Smith, *Lead with a Story*, 64.

## Chapter 13  Capture: The Artful Exchange of Value for Email Addresses

1. Sarah Austin, "Where Have All the Viners Gone?" *Entrepreneur*, May 24, 2018, https://www.entrepreneur.com/article/313038.

2. Caroline Forsey, "The Ultimate List of Email Marketing Stats for 2019," Hubspot, 2019, https://blog.hubspot.com/marketing/email-marketing-stats.

3. See 1 Timothy 6:10.

4. Jeff Walker, *Launch* (New York: Morgan James Publishing, 2014), 31.

## Chapter 14  Compile: Package Your Knowledge into Products and Services

1. Dan Miller with Michael Hyatt, "How to Make $150,000 This Year from Your Platform," *This Is Your Life* podcast, https://www.mixcloud.com/thisisyourlifewithmichaelhyatt/095-how-to-make-150000-this-year-from-your-platform-podcast.

2. Justine Tal Goldberg, "200 Million Americans Want to Publish Books, But Can They?," Publishing Perspectives, May 26, 2011, https://publishingperspectives.com/2011/05/200-million-americans-want-to-publish-books/.

3. Sia Mohajer, "The 3 Book Rule to Become an Expert," https://siamohajer.com/the-3-book-rule-of-being-an-expert.

## Chapter 15  Connect: How to Attract Your Audience to Your Message

1. Joseph Nicoletti, "What I Do," https://josephmichael.net/what-ido.

2. Dan Sullivan, "The Strategic Coach," https://private.strategiccoach.com/downloads/newsltr_i06_2000.pdf.

## Chapter 16  Encouraging Hearts: Moving People from Discouragement to Hope

1. Ben Melnyk, "The Power of Community in J. R. R. Tolkien's *The Lord of the Rings*," Lost and Found, April 4, 2016, https://nobodyunderstandslostandfound.wordpress.com/2016/04/04/the-power-of-community-in-j-r-r-tolkiens-the-lord-of-the-rings.

2. Diana Glyer, "C. S. Lewis, J. R. R. Tolkien, and the Inklings," C. S. Lewis, April 16, 2009, http://www.cslewis.com/c-s-lewis-j-r-r-tolkien-and-the-inklings.

3. John C. Maxwell, *Contagious Leadership Workbook*, the EQUIP Leadership Series (Nashville: Thomas Nelson, 2007), 71.

4. John Maxwell, *Everyone Communicates, Few Connect* (New York: HarperCollins Leadership, 2010), 64.

5. Richard L. Evans, *Richard Evans' Quote Book* (Salt Lake City: Publishers Press, 1971), 244.

6. "Products Larry Weiss Developed," Gort, https://gort.net/ProductIndex.htm.

## Chapter 17 Educating Heads: Moving People from Doubt to Confidence

1. Kary Oberbrunner, *Your Secret Name* (Grand Rapids: Zondervan, 2010).
2. "Kary Oberbrunner: Feeling the Pain," CBN, https://www1.cbn.com/700 club/kary-oberbrunner-feeling-pain.

## Chapter 18 Empowering Hands: Moving People from Delay to Action

1. E. F. Schumacher, quoted in Georgene Muller Lockwood, *The Complete Idiot's Guide to Simple Living* (Indianapolis: Alpha Books, 2000), 211.
2. Eugene Schwartz and Martin Edelston, *Breakthrough Advertising* (Boone, IA: Bottom Line Books, 2004).

## Chapter 19 The Messenger's Game Plan for Success

1. Nils Salzgeber, "Coach Wooden 35 Life Lessons," NJLifeHacks, https://www.njlifehacks.com/john-wooden-quotes-lessons.

**Jonathan Milligan** is an author, blogger, speaker, and online business coach. He is the creator of the popular weekly podcast and livestream show *Market Your Message*. Since 2009, Jonathan has run his own portable lifestyle business online. Today he teaches others how to build a business with their passion, story, or message. He lives in Jacksonville, Florida, with his wife, Charity, and their two kids, Kayla and Jordan. Visit JonathanMilligan.com for more information.

# CONNECT WITH
# Jonathan

# JonathanMilligan.com

 JonathanPMilligan

JonMilligan

 JonathanPMilligan

# *Want to Learn How to*
# MARKET YOUR MESSAGE?

Join Jonathan live each week for
the **Market Your Message** show!

You'll learn the latest tools, tips, and
strategies on how to increase the traffic,
leads, and sales of your business.

You can even binge-watch all of the past
episodes right now (it's free)!

**VISIT**
# MARKETYOURMESSAGE.COM/SHOW

Made in the USA
Columbia, SC
16 October 2020